Take Two CDs and Call Me in the Morning

2nd Edition

Suzanne E. Jonas, Ed.D.

ISBN 1-58961-473-9

Printed by:
48HrBooks.com
2249 14th St. S.W.
Akron, OH   44314
1-800-231-0521

CONTENTS

DEDICATION

For being a Christian and refusing to do sacrifice to Jupiter, Saint Cecilia was boiled in a bath tub, only to step out fragrant and refreshed; she was later swung at 3 times by a sword intended to lop off her head, which did not accomplish the task. She did die of these wounds 3 days later, but not before she completed many other acts of charity and conversion. She had the company of an angel throughout her life and converted many to Christianity. More than a thousand years after her death, a mistake in a Latin antiphon quotes her singing and playing an organ to God and this led to her becoming the figure of music. Her body was discovered in 1599 and re-interred with great pomp and circumstance. (She had been declared the patroness of music and all musical academies some years before). As a tribute to her, the feminine pronoun will be used throughout the text.

This book is dedicated to my parents: Evainez Beeler Jonas, who was a nurse, and Willard Reinhart Jonas, who was a public school instrumental music teacher. It took me over three decades to realize why I had chosen them for my parents!

PRELUDE

Without music my life would be empty! Music wakes me from the depths of sleep each morning, it keeps me calm during the commute to work, it focuses my attention and increases my concentration when working. I prescribe music to all of my patients, it accompanies my meals, my play, and eases me gently into the realms of dreams and alternate realities. I sing, dance, and play music - I love music. I love how it makes me feel - joyful, sacred, alive.

Music has been with me since I was born. Both of my parents played musical instruments and my father was a public school instrumental teacher. There was no way I was not going to learn how to play an instrument! By the sixth grade I was taking lessons on the flute, piano, violin, and oboe, spending what seemed like all of my waking life practicing and doing homework. I was in concert bands, dance bands, orchestras, choruses, woodwind quintets, small vocal ensembles, and even gave flute lessons to beginners when I was in high school. I was in solo and ensemble contests and won an international contest to perform in a marching band in the Rose Bowl Parade. My life was barreling full speed down the path of professional musician.

At eighteen I was awarded a position as 3rd flute/piccolo in a semiprofessional orchestra. It was wonderful sitting in the middle of all that incredible sound. Then, an interesting twist occurred in my musical career. During certain passages in a variety of pieces of music I would experience 'rushes' throughout my body that were so strong I could not play my flute! The feeling was very pleasant, but there were passages where I needed to perform, where the flute part was highlighted in the piece. What to do? I shared this with selected peers who did not know what I was talking about, but who suggested I learn how to control them, i.e. make the feelings disappear. Not realizing I was such a hedonist, I refused to control them. So, being a professional musician in an orchestra became less and less of an option. I went off to college and eventually became a public school instrumental teacher. That didn't last very long as I discovered I really didn't like teaching marching band.

Another twist of fate occurred much later when I was a doctoral student in Museum Studies. Isn't that a far cry from music!

Talking to a fellow graduate student one night at a party I was introduced to the new field of music therapy in medicine. It was if all my electrical circuits lit up at once. I spent the next month in the library researching this field with the result of changing my doctoral major to counseling psychology and creative therapies. It was also during this time I woke up to many forms of transpersonal psychology and realized the connection between my current choice of career and my parents: my mother was a nurse (medicine), and my father was a band teacher. MUSIC MEDICINE!

This book is the result of both personal experience and research into the healing aspects of music and sound. It is an ancient art being revived through modern technology. You can have music wherever you go thanks to batteries. There are CDs and techniques to assist you in healing mind, body, spirit and emotions. There are wonderful practitioners sounding tuning forks, bowls, frequencies, tones, songs, and music. It is a rich arena to explore and employ. I have had enormous breakthroughs in my own growth through the use of music and sound, and have had great good fun exploring all of the many ways we are using this modality for healing. My greatest pleasure is in using it with my patients and in teaching others the magic and power of music.

One thing to remember, though, as you explore for yourself the many avenues in Music and Sound Therapy: you do not need special speakers, bowls, flutes, or CDs to use music and sound for healing. All you need to do is

set an INTENT TO HEAL
then
HUM or SING

CHAPTER 1

WHAT IS MUSIC?

"Without music life would be a mistake".
Nietzsche

Since antiquity healers have written about music as a therapeutic agent. Music influences our mind and spirit, and it produces changes in our physiology as well as our emotions. We know that even the most ancient societies recognized how the daily experience of music contributed to the soul's growth. Specific music was recommended for healing, based upon musical form and instrumental timbres. We know, for example, about the ancient Sumerians (3000 B.C.) and their temple priests who spoke their oracles to an accompaniment of lyres. Their entreaties to the divinities for health were in the form of hymns. Although we have few descriptions of music or notes surviving from the Egyptian civilizations, a secret society, The Mysteries, used music extensively in chants, mantras, and invocations to obtain various emotional and spiritual results. We do know that they used seven vowel sounds to activate the energy centers of the body.

The power of music has played an important part in myths of every culture. In Greece, for example, Apollo is not only the god of healing, but also of music. In the Upanishads from India, the god Brahma uttered "OM" and out of this the universe came into being. Recent research has demonstrated that "when this syllable 'OM" is correctly intoned into a tonoscope (a device that transforms sounds into their visual representations on a screen), it produces a circle which is then filled in with concentric squares and triangles, finally producing, when the last traces of the 'mm' have died away, the Sri Yantra," the most revered of all Hindu geometric designs. (Jonathan Quintin, *Universal Symbols* in the CD Sri Yantra)

The ancient Hebrew writings are rich with references to music as a healing agent. Remember David's moving harp music that alleviated Saul's depression. Many songs are mentioned that are believed to protect against epidemics, and there is also note of a sleep inducing 'appliance:' water steadily dripping onto a metal place to create a monotonous buzz.   The Greek's use of music as a healing modality was inherited from earlier civilizations, but music therapy blossomed with the work of Pythagoras. A genius, this 6th century B.C. man who lived on the island of Samos, studied geometry in Egypt, astronomy from the Chaldeans, and philosophy from Zoroaster. In 530 B.C. he settled in Croton and established an academy. Here the students went through three levels all grounded in the notion that music is as high an art as mathematics. In Level 1, the Acoustici, you learned about various musical proportions and how to apply them. In Level II, the Mathematici, you learned about numbers, and mental self-control.   In the final Level III, the Electi, you learned the secret processes of psychic transmutation and healing with music and sound. There are no surviving writings of his, but we do know from his disciples and other writers that he was enigmatic, a mystic, a musician and mathematician with many followers. He exerted political influence, and taught a scientific view of the cosmos and interrelatedness of all human knowledge. His philosophy encompassed music, healing, science, mathematics, nutrition, and medicine and dominated the ancient world for 800 years!

The Pythagorean laws of music governed both the seen and unseen universe. According to these laws, the universe was founded and is governed by the laws of music: music made by man, unheard music made by each organism, and music made by the cosmos. If the universe was founded and governed by the laws of music, good music was in tune with the rhythm of life, and it was in harmony with the physiological activities of the healthy man. Concerning the healing qualities of music, Pythagoras taught his students that certain musical chords and melodies produce definite responses within the body. He also demonstrated that the right sequence of sounds played on an instrument could cure bodily pain, soothe the pangs of bereavement, calm anger, and still desire. And to approach the Divine, man could invoke the Spirit through music. Much of what Pythagoras taught is being revisited and proven as we use our modern technology. (Further discussion is in Chapter 7)

For musicians, Pythagoras discovered the arithmetical basis of musical intervals that we still use today. It was the first time that man discovered that universal truths could be explained through systematic investigation and use of symbols. (For a more complete and advanced discussion of this Lambdoma, I suggest starting at: www.lambdoma.com)

Hippocrates, the 'Father of Medicine', is said to have taken his patients who were suffering from mental illness to the Temple of Aesculapius (now in Turkey) where they would listen to the stirring music. At this time, music was considered as high an endeavor as science and a builder of one's character. Paracelsus practiced what he called a 'musical medicine'. Here specific compositions were played for specific maladies, be they mental, moral, or physical. It is interesting to note that the Roman temple priests and physicians practiced music therapy until their function was discredited as the Empire became completely Christianized.

Medieval physicians often employed minstrels to speed recovery of convalescing patients, but, for the most part, the ancient art of healing with music seems to have vanished across Europe during this time. We do know of one 16th century physician, Baptista Porta, who prescribed lutes of various woods to cure dropsy, sciatica, and fainting, revealing that at least a thin strain of music therapy had survived.

With the development of Cartesian science, based on Rene' DeCartes theory that only information gleaned from the five senses was valid, all therapeutic practices involving the spirit or emotions were erased from 'modern' European medicine. These most basic, traditional healing modalities were relegated to shamans, faith healers, and medicine men. Today the therapeutic potential of music is therefore difficult for us 'rational' Western thinkers to perceive or even imagine. Apart from a few exceptional instances, music therapy is not in wide institutional use today. Because of music's intangibility and widespread use, most people and scientists do not consider music capable of producing significant healing effects.

However, a walk through any large bookstore or search on the web will reveal that something has shifted. There are now many books on various aspects of music and sound therapies and healing, and many web sites devoted to promoting a variety of music/sound healing techniques and CDs. (see Appendix C) Researchers and practitioners are delving into these areas to prove what the Ancients knew: playing music, toning, chanting, and listening to music and sound can have healing effects on our mind, body, emotions, and spirit.

What is this thing called "music"?

In an attempt to define this ephemeral phenomena I have collected a wide variety of definitions of music through the years. The following are just a few, starting with one from *The American Heritage Dictionary.*

The art of organizing sound so as to elicit
an aesthetic response in a listener

Other definitions include:

Music is an activity, something done, an experience lived through by
composer, performer and listener.

After silence, that which comes nearest to expressing the inexpressible is
music. Aldous Huxley

Music is emotion in sound.

Music is the art of sound.

In short, music is organized sound; and sound is vibration. Quantum physics demonstrates that all matter is composed of one basic substance or energy, and each living and nonliving thing is a unique vibrating system determined by characteristic frequencies of vibration or rhythm. Scientists at Yale University have observed that the planets in our solar system emit distinct sounds created by their magnetospheric waves (vibrations). Apparently, Saturn hums a slow, dreamy melody; Mercury has a chirping, quick silvery sound; and the Sun radiates 80 different overtones! NASA has actual recordings of some of the planets from the Voyager space program. (*Celestial Harmonies* CD by Jeffery Thompson) This finding substantiates the sixth century B.C. teaching of Pythagoras, who called this effect the "Harmony of the Spheres". He also calculated the mathematical ratios between the vibratory rates of notes, and stated that these ratios reflect a universal law of harmony that describes planetary motions, the basic law of music, and the inner life of the soul. (www.lambdoma.com)

Music, then, is audible, organized vibration. The vibrations that constitute music differ from the random and irregular vibrations of noise. A pure tone creates a regular, evenly timed sine wave that repeats itself. Remember your experience with the oscilloscope? To demonstrate the "clarity" of tones, the eighteenth-century German physicist Ernst Chladni scattered sand on a metal plate and drew a violin bow across the edge of the plate. The sand scattered into astonishing symmetrical geometric shapes. Chladni's work remained in the realm of curiosity until the twentieth century, when Swiss scientist Hans Jenny filmed the instantaneous shaping effects of tones (This is discussed in Chapter 7). So, even though we may criticize a piece of music as "noise", if the tones used in the composition have regular sine waves, then it is, indeed, music; disconcerting and painful to listen to maybe, but still, technically, music.

How Music is Organized

The most basic tool to organize audible vibrations is **PULSE or BEAT**. This is the part of music to which you tap your foot. It is the regular division of time that defines music. Most western music is divided into groups of 2, 3, 4, or 6 beats, each grouping called a measure. Marches are in 2 beat measures, waltzes are in 3 beats to a measure, and hymns are generally 4 beats to a measure. An interesting phenomenon is that the first beat of every grouping (2, 3, 4 or 6) is the strongest.

RHYTHM is the recurrence of long and short patterns of notes. Think of the cha-cha dance. The basic rhythm is: **one-two-cha**-cha-**cha**. The beat falls on one, two, and then the first and last cha. In the broadest sense, beat and rhythm are the organizing principals of our world and our lives: heartbeats, breathing, cycle of days and nights, seasons, and the march of years.

When a succession of tones used in a meaningful way is added to rhythm, this becomes **MELODY**. Usually it is the first thing people in Western society hear in a piece of music, unless the rhythm is overpowering. It is the 'tune' that we whistle or hum or join with words. Perhaps melody corresponds to our thoughts--- both are linear, have a beginning, middle, and an end, and exist singularly.

Melody and rhythm together have been the natural components of music from the earliest of times. When a different (non-melodic) note was added to a song, then **HARMONY** was born. The effect was to add depth and richness and is a relatively recent phenomenon in western music. Harmony was probably introduced to canonical forms in the ninth century, when monks added a second line of notes sung parallel to the original melody. Most harmony is tonal; it centers around a 'key note' which gives music a feeling of being centered and finished at its conclusion. Some twentieth century composers, however, devised systems that do not have a central tone. This music never quite sounds as if it comes to rest.

When three or more tones are combined simultaneously, we refer to the structure as a chord. Some chords are pleasant, peaceful and stable; these are consonant, and easy to listen to. Dissonant chords are somewhat disconcerting, agitating, and unstable; they demand resolution into a pleasing chord. Pieces of music that contain a majority of dissonant chords are difficult to listen to unless there is periodic resolution to consonant chords --- to peace. Most traditional music uses dissonance with caution, but it is important to use some so the music will be interesting. Harmony corresponds with our various emotions and with the harmonious workings of the body systems. These, too, can be consonant or dissonant, as in mental or physical illnesses.

The last basic element of music is **TEMPO**, the overall speed of performance. The composer most often provides a marking to assist the performers. This is correlated to a system of beats per minute. Often composers or editors will provide an indication like: quarter note =78. One can use a metronome and easily find the suggested tempo. During the piece, the tempo most likely will vary. Terms are added to tell the performers when and where, i.e. 'accelerando' under the notes means a gradual quickening of the music. Tempo in music is most like our overall energy: laid back, energetic, erratic, low. We also determine our own 'tempo' in heartbeats per minute by taking our pulse. If we want to raise or lower our pulse by listening to music, all we need do is use a piece of music that is higher or lower in tempo than our own pulse, and our body will attempt to match the tempo, especially if we have ingested any type of mind altering drug or pharmaceutical. (Music's effects on the body will be more fully discussed in Chapter 5.)

A further quality of music is **TIMBRE**, or tone color. This is the characteristic quality of the sound produced by a voice or instrument. A cello has a timbre very different from a trombone, though both can play the identical notes. A melody sung by the opera singer Lucianno Pavarotti will sound very different when performed by popular folk singer James Taylor. The quality of the sound is dependent upon the material from which an instrument is made, its size and shape, and many smaller variables, such as the diameter or thickness of the tubing, or a string instrument's sounding board.

The instruments producing the sound are grouped together in families. String instruments produce sound through the vibration of thin strings by either plucking, bowing, strumming, or striking. These include: violins, violas, cellos, string bass, guitars, harp, and piano. The woodwind family includes both wood and metal instruments that produce sound by blowing and covering holes with fingers or keys. Examples include flute, clarinet, oboe, bassoon, and saxophone. The brass family includes the trumpet, French horn, trombone, baritone, and tuba. Brass sounds are produced by buzzing the lips into a cup shaped mouthpiece and pushing down valves, or in the case of the trombone, moving a slide. The fourth family, percussion, contains a wide variety of struck or shaken instruments: drums, bells, piano, maracas, tambourine, and many others.

In order to fully understand music as therapy, it is extremely important to have some general knowledge of the history of music within a culture and the different styles of classical music. This is no different, in my opinion, than learning about the different drugs that a medical person may administer to a patient. The more one understands the 'product', the better able one is to make informed decisions regarding administration and treatment. The Appendix contains a basic outline of Western classical music. I suggest borrowing tapes/CDs from the local library or friends to become acquainted with the vast riches of our musical heritage. Above all else

ENJOY!

CHAPTER 2

MUSIC AS THERAPY

The man that hath no music in himself,
Nor is not moved with concord of sweet sounds...
The motions of his spirit are dull as night...
Wm. Shakespeare, "The Merchant of Venice"

The prevailing model of healing for Western civilization was established in the nineteenth century with the discovery of germs as a cause of disease, and the rigorous, scientific study of a variety of physical illnesses as the core discipline. This medical model categorically analyzes the negative, unhealthy state relative to norms of cholesterol accumulation, blood pressure number, germ invasion, etc. The physician is trained to react primarily, if not exclusively, to quantitative information displayed by the illness, and to treat both the symptoms and the perceived physical cause. Under the model, since the patient has no medical training, she is dependent upon the authority of the professional to heal her through drugs and/or surgery. Health practitioners have envisioned the body as a machine in good or bad repair. If a body is in bad condition, the practitioner views the pain and disease as negative and attempts to 'repair or cure' the ailing machine.

A challenge to this model arose during the 1960s when American culture was experiencing a great social turbulence: existing institutions were strongly criticized for their impotence and inability to deal with mounting problems. The concerns, values, behavior, and music of the countercultures were rapidly assimilated. The 1970s witnessed the emergence of the Human Potential movement, whose philosophy emphasized the integrated, actualized self as the means and purpose of existence: know yourself, develop yourself, and become independent of others. Although this was a separatist philosophy it was one that promoted individual growth. The reliance on authorities began to erode as people began to claim responsibility for them selves. A direct result was the examination of the old institutions of education and medicine. In the 1980s the search for self discovered that mind

19

and body are not separate, but constantly acting upon one another: the Cartesian view of a divided mind and body was being reversed. Researchers began to prove that ratings of emotional health are directly predictive of physical health, that physical health can be affected by thoughts and emotions. Now patients and professionals alike are beginning to see beyond symptoms to the context of illness: society, family, stress, diet, emotions, and most importantly, beliefs.

Holistic Medicine

The holistic, or wholistic, model represents the interaction of mind, body, emotions, spirit, and environment. It seeks to correct the underlying disharmony causing the problem by viewing pain and disease as external manifestations of internal conflict and disharmony. Unlike the medical doctor, the holistic healer acts as a therapeutic partner with the patient to change dissonant patterns that promote disease. These patterns might be in diet, interpersonal relationships, work, and belief systems. A variety of treatments such as therapeutic touch, visualization, biofeedback, hypnosis, holophonics, mindfulness meditation, energy therapies and music are employed. These new ways to achieve self-healing are being explored by both patients and progressive medical professionals as they attempt to incorporate them with conventional practice. Known as CAM therapies, Complimentary and Alternative Medicine, their usage is spreading as people are seeking to supplement or go beyond allopathic medicine and drugs. John Cabot Zin, Ph.D. was one of the pioneers at the University of Massachusetts Medical School. His highly successful meditation program for patients with a variety of medically diagnosed symptoms, Mindfulness Meditation, is now being taught in many hospitals and healthcare centers. The results speak for themselves: patients are able to reduce physical symptoms and lead more fulfilling lives by taking the time to be mindful.

The holistic concept of health is gaining more support as it becomes legitimized by federal and state programs, endorsed by politicians, urged by insurance companies, and adopted by many hospitals, medical practitioners, and students of healing. After decades of trying to explain one mystery after another through science, at least some are now coming to terms with the unavoidable and critical influence of the patient's expectations and experiences. The mood of the hospital staff, the physical environment, the fame of the medical center, and honest communication between staff and patient are important aspects of health care beginning to be more fully recognized. A 1992 article in the *New England Journal of Medicine* surveyed Americans' healthcare choices. One of every three Americans in 1990 was using 'unconventional' therapies for illness, spending $14 million in the process. A third of these were going to see alternative practitioners: 72% were not telling their doctors about their other therapists. All told, Americans had made more visits to alternative therapists, 425 million, than they had to all types of primary care physicians, 388 million. Given these facts, in 1992 the Senate Appropriations Committee directed the National Institutes of Health to explore "the potential that exists in unconventional medical practices," and gave them a $2 million grant to do so. The Office of Alternative Medicine (OAM) was established to study these philosophies and techniques. Since that time there have been studies on acupuncture, homeopathy, guided imagery, yoga, massage, macrobiotics, touch and energy healing, Tai Chi, Ayurveda, and the effects of prayer. There have also been numerous physicians, Dr. Andrew Weil for one, who have embraced the concept of alternative and complementary medicine and promoted it whole- heartedly.

The federal government subsequently established the National Center for Complementary and Alternative Medicine (NCCAM) within the National Institutes of Health to both research and disseminate information on CAM therapies (http://nccam.nih). The most comprehensive and reliable findings to date on Americans' use of CAM were released in May 2004 by the NCCAM[1] and Center for Disease Control. The results of that survey show 36% of adults were using some form of CAM. The survey included provider-based therapies, such as acupuncture and chiropractic, and other therapies that do not require a provider, such as natural products, special diets, and megavitamin therapy. It also included prayer. It did not include music therapy. Overall, the survey showed CAM use is greater by: women than men; people with higher education levels; people who have been hospitalized in the past year; and former smokers.

The interest in Complementary and Alternative Medicine and whole systems of health care among the public, patients, health care practitioners, researchers, industry, and government regulators continues to grow. This growth has been accompanied by an increasing amount of research and publication of articles in the mainstream bio-medical journals as well as CAM journals. There are a number of highly specialized journals that deal with different forms of

CAM practices, such as acupuncture, chiropractic, homeopathic, Chinese medicine, and other ethnic herbal medicinal practices. Currently, there are eight general CAM journals: Complementary Therapies in Medicine (CTM), Complementary Therapies in Nursing & Midwifery, BMC Complementary and Alternative Medicine, Focus on Alternative and Complementary Therapies from UK; Alternative Medicine Reviews, Alternative Therapies in Health and Medicine (ATHM), Journal of Alternative and Complementary Medicine (JACM) from USA; and Complementary Medicine (CMR) from Switzerland.

Twentieth Century Music Therapy

Ironically, wars have been a major influence in bringing the use of music back as a healing agent in the twentieth century. The initial application of music was in veterans' hospitals, where it gradually evolved along two main lines:

1) as an addition to physical therapy, with music prescribed to accompany exercise for joints and muscles, and with blowing an instrument to increase the use of the lungs and larynx; singing was also recommended along with instrument playing.

2) as an adjunct to psychiatric treatment, to promote socialization, tension-reduction, diversion, self-expression, and imagery.

Through the U.S. Army's reconditioning program, music therapy was implemented in Veterans' Administration Hospitals by medical officers in the early twentieth century. This program exposed musicians and administrators to the potentials of music in a hospital setting, helped increase the understanding of the functional uses of music, and led to the establishment of Music Therapy as a profession.

By the late 1960s the two most commonly shared goals of practicing music therapists were:

1) the patients' establishment or reestablishment of relationships, and,

2) the achievement of self-esteem through self actualization.

These goals for patients in mental institutions are approached through participation in music making and through listening and responding to music. A great deal of research supports the healing effects of music on the spirit and emotions of the mentally ill.

In an atmosphere of suppression resulting from inflexible regimens, public prejudice, narrow-minded traditions and the weight of the mental hospital organization, the task of healing becomes all but impossible. Music is capable of counteracting much of the fear, restraint, and loneliness: it allows for emotional freedom and validation of the ego, and for a feeling of unity and belonging. [2]

The other line along which music therapy evolved, as adjunct to physical therapy, developed in hospitals for the physically and mentally handicapped. Here, the actual production of music, singing, and playing musical instrument has had tremendous influence on the total mind/body/spirit of the autistic patient, the mentally retarded, physically impaired, learning disabled, and brain damaged. According to researcher Arthur Harvey [3], the strength of such therapy with these populations lies in music's ability to increase verbal and nonverbal interaction, increase psychomotor patterns, develop coordination, establish rapport and promote confidence. He states: "I know of no other educational process that can involve and integrate the cognitive [mind], affective [emotional], and psychomotor [body] domains of the personality in the meeting of physiological, security, safety, belongingness, and esteem needs as effectively as music can."

Current Music Therapy

The American Music Therapy Association (www.musictherapy.org) defines music therapy as an established healthcare profession that uses music to address physical, emotional, cognitive, and social needs of individuals of all ages. Music therapy improves the quality of life for persons who are well and meets the needs of children and adults with disabilities or illnesses. Music therapy interventions can be designed to: promote wellness, manage stress, alleviate pain, express feelings, enhance memory, improve communication, and promote physical rehabilitation. From this list we see that music is indeed a holistic therapy, one that affects mind, body, emotions, and spirit. Subsequent chapters will address each of these areas.

The practice of music therapy today is divided into two principal schools:

　　1) that which seeks to work through listening; and

　　2) that which would bring help to the patients through their own involvement in making music.

Behind these two approaches lie two very different philosophies. The first group, which seeks change through listening, is composed of Freudians, Jungians, Transpersonalists, and bioacousticians who are concerned with anxiety reduction, healing, catharsis, sublimation, changes in emotional and physiological states, and the process of self-actualization/realization/fulfillment through music. They place their faith in the spiritual and biophysical powers of music. The second group maintains that music is capable of curing a patient through active musical experience. These behaviorists tend to use music to change behavior through participation, i.e., music becomes therapeutic when it is physically and emotionally related to by the patient while singing, performing, or exercising.

The tremendous value of music, as we shall explore in further chapters, is precisely its ability to simultaneously influence the mind, body, spirit, and emotions. Used regularly, music is an effective outlet for feelings of stress incurred in our daily lives. In times of intense emotional crisis, music can assist us in clarifying issues and liberating our responses by bringing about a degree of emotional catharsis. When symptoms do appear, carefully selected music can help to decrease their severity and increase the body's own healing mechanisms, thereby easing the pain and anguish. And music that touches our spirits can assist us in both transcending and transforming emotional and physical suffering.

There are numerous articles in magazines and journals on the effectiveness of music as a healing agent and there are many books and websites exploring this ancient modality. (See Appendix C) Because of the cheap technology of radios, CD players, speakers, and MP3 players and the proliferation of recorded music, we need never be without our music. However, to be used effectively as a healing modality, there are several things to consider.

For as Shakespeare said: "**Music is a double edged sword**".

---

[1]Barnes P, Powell-Griner E, McFann K, Nahin R. *CDC Advance Date Report #343.* Complimentary and alternative medicine use among adults: United States, 2002. May 27, 2004.

[2]Altshuler, Ira. "The Organism-as-a-Whole and Music Therapy". in Podolsky, E. Music Therapy. N.Y.: Philosophical Library. 1954.

[3]Harvy, A. "The Therapeutic Role of Music in Special Education." Creative Child and Adult Quarterly: 3(3), 196-204. 1980.

CHAPTER 3

EFFECTS OF MUSIC ON THE EMOTIONS AND MIND

The final frontier is not outer space, but inner space.
Edgar Mitchell, Astronaut

The Mind/Body Connection

Thanks to modern technology and the important work of biologist researcher Candace Pert (*Molecules of Emotion, 1997*), most medical doctors and psychologists and a growing number of lay people, now accept that emotions are a major factor in the development of illness. Research demonstrates that emotions that are not expressed directly produce physical symptoms. Originally termed 'psychosomatic', symptoms such as headaches, 'butterflies in the stomach', and eczema were accepted empirically as being mentally produced. The list of such symptoms is growing as the connections are being clinically documented. The University of Massachusetts Medical Center Stress Clinic has a checklist for their patients listing ninety-nine stress symptoms.

Not only does suppressing emotions channel stress to weaker parts of the body to produce symptoms, but growing evidence supports the connection between prolonged perceived stress and major chemical changes in the body, e.g., triggering of cancer cells, changes in the body's immune function, changes in the chemical make up of certain organs. Research by Peter Guy Manners in the area of vibrational medicine (see more in Chapter 7) is attempting to demonstrate that vibrational change in the body is due to repressed emotion. Whenever we experience such feeling of anger, grief, helplessness, dispair, hopelessness, the frequencies of our organs change. Such change might result in, for example, a diseased liver --- one that is of a different vibratory rate than a healthy liver, i.e. one that is 'out of tune'.

A perfect example of this mind/body connection is my own personal experience while traveling in Turkey. A group of teenagers approached my husband and I while walking through an Istanbul park. They convinced my husband to buy a travel guide book of the city.

Alarms went off in my head that told me not to buy this. But the three of them were talking so fast and creating so much confusion, that I handed over the money. As we were walking away I figured out that we had just paid $25 for a twenty page booklet! I was so furious, not at them, but at myself for not listening to my intuition and saying 'no' to them. I could feel that anger in every cell of my body. That night I became really sick. And I stayed sick in bed for three days, missing several sites I really had wanted to see. As soon as I forgave myself, I began to recover. This was a fast, no holds barred demonstration of the power of my anger to diminish my immune system.

Behavioral Medicine is a line of psychology based in this belief that all physical symptoms are nothing more than a manifestation of unresolved emotional conflicts. As writer Carolyn Myss states: "Your Issues are in your Tissues". The Behavioral Medicine psychologist focuses on finding the emotional antecedent to the physical symptom by using biofeedback, relaxation training, and in-depth psychological interventions to address behavior and belief structures. Examples of such connections are: anger and heart disease, hostility and cancer. Behavioral Medicine reminds us that *The Only Opponent is Within.*

Dr. Alfred Tomatis discovered that we selectively tune out sounds associated with trauma. For example, a man who was consistently yelled at by his father and told never to look away from him when he was yelling, had several missing frequencies in his voice patterns. When he went through intensive Tomatis Therapy (more on this in Chapter 6), he began to hear male voices more clearly and could hear his own voice for the first time, not even realizing that this hearing had been obstructed. He had noticed that making male friends was difficult. Tomatis also found that many Jewish people who survived WW II, were deaf in the frequency of the sirens of the trucks that took them to death camps.

As can be seen from the above examples, to stay healthy it is most important that you release powerful emotions before they settle into your cells, change frequency rates, and become dis-ease.

Music and the Emotions

A piece of music comes on the radio. What is your first reaction to it? 'I like it'; "Turn it off"; "Yuk"; "You call that music?" We are so judgmental based upon our emotional response to the music.

Music therapist C. D. Kenny[1] views music as a resource pool that contains images, patterns, mood suggestions, textures, feelings and processes. Great leaders and religions have relied upon this emotional response to music to arouse and unite followers. One need only remember being in church singing a rousing hymn such as "Onward Christian Soldiers" or a Christmas carol such as "Silent Night" to understand the effect on emotions. At parades and band concerts, the marches stir the heart and arouse pride and spirit. Most countries incorporate an instrumental ensemble into their armed forces to assist in arousing their fighting and national spirit.

Shamans and medicine men and women of all tribes and civilizations have utilized music, chanting, or drumming to create an atmosphere of heightened emotion in which to heal. In these situations, the music, usually drumming, helps center one's attention on the ritual and intent and intensify the feelings of the participants. For the healer, the sounds help in shifting consciousness from sensory to spiritual energies for healing.

Writers have also extolled the virtues of music for quieting or arousing the soul. Composers and musicians themselves have described the ability of music to alter their moods.

I love music passionately...It is a free art gushing forth, an open air art boundless as the elements, the wind, the sky, the sea... Music is the expression of the movement of the waters, the play of curves described by changing breezes.
Claude Debussy\

Mood Alteration

One of the first modern recorded studies that examined the psychological effects of music was in 1890 by Dr. W. T. Weimner. Piano music was played to 1400 mentally ill women. By observing the patients, he found that rhythm had no effect except when it evoked memories, and that slow music soothed the more severely ill. Many other researchers concur with Weimner's study in stressing the important of tempo. In her research, psychologist Kate Hevner[2] determined that tempo and rhythm (dotted figures or uneven patterns) were equally important in shaping an emotional state, but melody was not significant. Esther Gatewood[3], another psychologist and researcher, said rhythm is the chief factor in arousing the feelings of happiness and excitement. And since then many researchers have noted that exciting music produces more anxiety and aggression and increases worry and emotionality. It would appear that rhythm is the element of music that has the most effect on one's physiology (see Chapter 5) and emotions. It is not until the listener has the capacity or willingness to experience music in greater depth that the other factors of music --- melody, harmony, tone color --- develop increased importance and effect. A good example of this can be seen in children. They love music with strong rhythms; and we have all been blasted with teenager's stereos whose speakers are vibrating and gyrating with the rhythms of their music.

Personnel in psychiatric hospitals have consistently made use of the above responses to music. Caretakers have found music will significantly assist in changing the moods of patients in large wards, thereby decreasing dependence on drugs and increasing the pleasure of the patients. Ira Altshuler, a well-known music therapist researcher, discovered that to alter the moods of these patients effectively, the music used must first match the mood of the patient. For example, if the patient is angry, the music must first be of an 'angry' mood or tempo in order to gain the patient's attention and connect emotionally. Certainly, when a person is very angry, playing a sweet lullaby will not serve to calm her. It will be more likely to aggravate. It appears that only after the patient has worked herself "musically into the mood or tempo of the music can a shift to a different mood or tempo be made."[4] This has come to be known as the 'iso principle': matching the mood of the patient with the music. Then the process of shifting or altering moods takes place, by allowing the strong emotion to be cathartic or worked out, and then playing music closer to the desired mood. Psychologist Larry Shatin[5] working with college students, used the term 'vectoring' to designate this shift. The moods he 'vectored' through music were:

sad/depressed	to	gay/happy
restless/agitated	to	serene/tranquil
bored/restless	to	active/alert
active/alert	to	majestic/exalted

While these researchers concentrated on using music to alter moods, others were ascertaining the moods of particular pieces of music. In 1937, psychologist Kate Hevner had tested many musical selections as to their elicited moods, finding high percentages of agreement between normal populations. She developed a 'Mood

28

Wheel' as a result of her study. Her system for classifying the emotional expression of musical selections arranged sixty-six adjectives in a circle of eight related groups. The mood clusters are arranged in such a way that adjacent groups are closely related to each other and opposite groups are unlike. Subsequent researchers who have utilized this wheel confirm the universality of moods to some musical selections. The selections in the appendix of this book represent music with universal mood agreement.

MOOD WHEEL

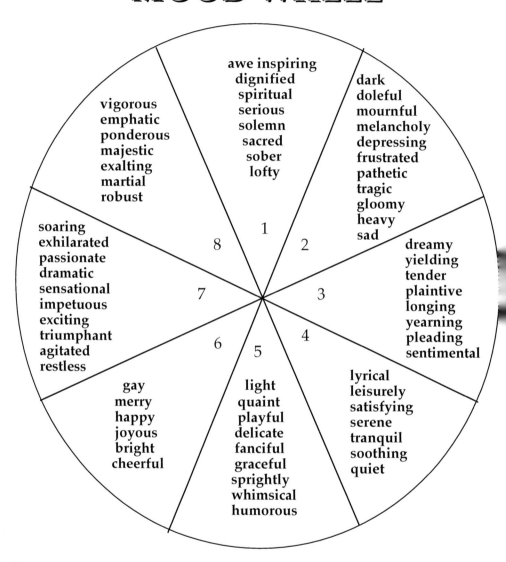

Kate Hevner, 1937

To alter or change a mood, first locate on the mood wheel the current emotional state. Does the person feel she is sad (2), yearning (3), agitated (7)? Then ask for a level of intensity of that emotion on a scale of 1-10 where 10 represents the maximum. How sad is she on a scale of 1-10? If she is more than 6, play a piece of music that will elicit her sadness, for instance Barber's *Adagio for Strings* or Sibelius' *Swan of Tuonela*, both powerful in evoking tears, which are the body's mechanism for releasing sadness and grief. Once the emotion has been released, consider where you would like to be on the mood wheel. Perhaps trying to be humorous and playful (5) after crying is just too far from sad (2). It might be better to 'vector' around the wheel and move just to quiet and soothing (4). An appropriate selection that elicits an uplifting calm and peace is the second movement of Beethoven's 6th symphony, an incredibly beautiful and loving piece of music. Just prior to writing this symphony, Beethoven accepted the painful reality that he was losing his precious hearing. (See *Beethoven's Hair,* a real page-turner, for insight into his state of emotion and the likely cause of his deafness.) The music reflects his acceptance and willingness to continue to allow music to flow through him for others. It therefore has the power to allow listeners to accept whatever tragic event is currently shaping their life and then to move on through it. The third and fourth movements are very positive and full of hope and renewal.

By using this primary response to music, we can effectively release and transform those emotions that can trigger dis-ease.

Creativity

For most people the subject of creativity brings up pictures of flower arrangements or oil paintings. Years of research in creativity have shown it to be a multifaceted phenomenon with many expressions. These range from simple problem solving, which all of us do everyday, to the expressions of the collective unconscious evidenced in the work of the visionary artists and musicians.

The literature on creativity describes four distinct levels:

1) First Level creativity involves making a slight change to an idea or concept or object. Examples of this might include changing one's shoe laces, rearranging anything, trimming hair, or growing a mustache.

2) Second Level creativity consists of adding another item to the original while still maintaining the integrity of the original. This would be an innovation such as adding decoration to something: icing a cake; embellishing a story; adding harmony to a melody; or it could

be a partly new item with the original features modified sufficiently to be perceived as different in detail though not in essence, e.g., clock radio, hooded sweatshirt, jumpsuit.

3) Third Level creativity combines two factors to achieve a completely new item. Examples of this include the combining of chemicals or metals; making a cake from flour, sugar and butter; collage art; and using heat on sand to make glass.

4) Fourth Level creativity marks the appearance of an essentially new item. Examples from science are 'manmade' elements such as plutonium and einsteinium. In art it is the totally new concept in music like the Serial system played on new instruments. New technologies such as radio or microwave cooking are also examples.

At the most basic level, people are producing creatively all the time. It is a natural instinct and program of living things. It exists in every individual in both physical and mental activities, only awaiting proper conditions to be released and expressed. Professor Doris Shallcross, a leading researcher in the area of creative behavior [6,] has demonstrated that creativity can be elicited from any and everyone, if the environment is conducive. Creative ambiance is established and characterized by flexible attitude in the subject and other individuals involved; an expressive situation and tools for expression; and spontaneous play with patterns, shapes, and sounds: in other words, an openness to experience and the right climate in which to take risks.

By using the inherent qualities of music --- the ability to bypass the ego, ability to calm the physiology, foster imagery, release repressed psychological material, pleasure, and mood --- one's creativity can be stimulated. To enhance brainstorming sessions, in the background play one of these hemi-sync CDs: *Illumination, Masterworks,* or *Baroque Garden**. To stimulate artistic production, try the exercise explained below under Imagery & Music.

Imagery & Music

After our initial response to a piece of music, most people have images that are stimulated by the notes: memories, or new images. Researchers have noted an overall consistency of imagery 'types' per piece of music among a variety of populations. For instance, while listening to Schumman's *When Jesus Wept*, most listeners have images of death in such forms as funerals, coffins, destruction after war. Another example would be images of expansion---outer space, flying, spiritual experiences---that many people report experiencing while listening to Holst's *Neptune* from *The Planets Suite*.

Exercise - Try listening to any of the selections listed in Appendix A under "Imagery Producing Music". These pieces of music are particularly effective at stimulating images.

1. Get into a comfortable position, focus on your breathing two minutes allowing yourself to relax and breathe deeper and deeper.

2. Using stereo headphones, or resting between two good stereo speakers, turn on the music and let the music guide your imagination. If nothing comes to mind right away, ask yourself what the music reminds you of, and go from there. Allow the images to flow, like a movie, without analyzing them.

3. Afterwards, use the images to stimulate ideas for a poem, story, painting, dance, or song. You might also relate these images to any problem in your daily life. The images will usually be metaphors whose meanings will need to be unlocked.

Universality of Mood and Image

Music-stimulated imagery can help one learn more about oneself; this can be a useful part of a process of problem solving, goal setting, or attainment.

Music's ability to bypass the ego, our chief censor, activates the more unconscious levels of the psyche. Carl Jung identified this universality of images as the 'collective unconscious', an area where each individual's psyche connects with all other psyches. In the collective unconscious reside archetypal images, primal images that are the models or building blocks for all others. Art historians and archeologists have found the same basic symbols in primitive art all over the world, even in cultures just recently touched by modern man. There is such a thing as archetypal music, too. Children in all cultures sing the same six- note phrase during their early years. This is the phrase they use when defying others: nah nah nah nah naaaaaaaah nah.

In order to use music to learn about oneself ,it is very important to be RELAXED before beginning the process. The more conscious one is, the more 'in the world' one's thoughts are: busy, active, and involved with events and people. As a person begins to relax, she shifts her consciousness; if she relaxes to the point of falling asleep, she dreams. It is, however, possible to relax completely *without* falling asleep. This is a state of "mind awake, body asleep" where individual imagination and imagery mix with the collective unconscious. This is a quiet state in which conscious thoughts are not intrusive, and in which the mind does not pursue thoughts and impressions.

Exercise: To begin the relaxation process for this exercise, try the following:

1) chant a mantra or the universal 'om' for 10-15 minutes.

2) imagine a room where you leave all thoughts and feelings, closing and locking the heavy door as you leave.

3) do progressive relaxation: very slowly fix your attention on each part of your body, starting with your toes and moving up, noticing where you are tense, and easing those muscles and joints; OR

4) actually tense the muscles, hold the tension, then release, starting at your toes and moving slowly up to your scalp.

5) When you are relaxed, imagine a beautiful, sparkling colored light entering a hole in the top of your head and **slowly** filling every part of you, down to your toes. Imagine that wherever the light goes, it changes you in some way, making you more relaxed, warmer, more healthy, and so on.

6) Then, imagine yourself in a meadow or forest. Allow yourself to note details in your environment: plants, animals, geography, sky, time of day, time of year, air on your skin, and smells. When you are ready, turn on the music and let the music guide you in your meadow or forest, or let it take you wherever it will.

7) When finished, write down everything you can remember in as much detail as possible.

8) Perhaps you might be inspired to draw a picture, paint, or write a story or poem. This can be a tremendous tool for creative production. Later, reconsider your experience. This is a metaphor for your daily life --- it is up to you to decipher it. And it may reveal a completely different explanation in a month as you begin to see yourself. Look for patterns, see characters as aspects of yourself, imagine a conversation with them and record it in your journal. Whatever you do with this useful practice, HAVE FUN. This modality can be explored further with therapists trained in the technique called Guided Imagery and Music (see Chapter 4).

Aural Development and Music Brain Research

In his research on the human brain, Harvard scientist Howard Gardner concluded that it is the musical/sound portion of the child's cognition that develops first, and that it is an important area to stimulate fully, since succeeding areas to be developed build upon the aural center. Music educators in England have long emphasized aural development in their schools. They realize that as the child develops various forms of thinking - reasoning, intuition, creativity, memorization, and judgment - these are accompanied by auditory perception. This becomes the foundation for later work in verbal language, and then reading and writing. Their emphasis in the early years, therefore, is to develop greater auditory perception. By listening to sounds and observing what goes on around them, children learn to express what they hear, see, and feel. They will then write and speak clearly and develop various kinds of thinking such as linear, spatial, musical, or verbal more easily.

At the 1994 American Psychological Assn. convention, a University of California research team reported that their music listening experiments with preschool children demonstrated a causal link between music and spatial reasoning. Spatial reasoning tasks involve the orientation of shapes in space. Such tasks are relevant to a wide range of endeavors, from higher mathematics and geometry to architecture, engineering, drawing and playing chess. The group of three year olds received eight months of special music training consisting of daily group singing lessons, weekly private lessons on electronic keyboards and daily keyboard practice and play. Scores on a spatial reasoning task improved dramatically after the music lessons. Other research also points to the advanced abilities of students who take music lessons. They tend to exceed the national average SAT scores by 51 points on verbal, and 39 on math.

The U.C. researchers also reported on an effect with 12 college undergraduates who listened to Mozart's *Sonata for Two Pianos in D* for 10 minutes and then had to solve visual puzzles. The important subtest of the Stanford-Binet test was a paper folding and cutting task. The subjects had to imagine that a single sheet of paper has been folded several times and then various cut outs are made with a scissors. The task is to correctly predict the pattern of cut outs when the paper was unfolded. Those students who listened to Mozart scored an average of 8 points higher than control groups who were given relaxation instructions or simply sat in silence. The press immediately proclaimed that Mozart made you smarter and it became known as the Mozart Effect. Two critical and highly limiting factors were generally ignored: first, that the effects were not on general intelligence but only for a test of spatial abilities; and second, the effects lasted only a few minutes! Since that time, there have been many research studies focusing on this Mozart effect with the result that there is no agreement about whether or not the Mozart Effect is genuine.[7]

Over the years, various other curious Mozart research anecdotes have surfaced: cows serenaded with Mozart give more milk; Mozart string quartets played in the city squares in Edmonton, Canada decrease drug dealings; and in northern Japan, Ohara Brewery finds that Mozart makes the best sake. Apparently the density of the yeast used for brewing increases by a factor of ten.

Mozart's music scores another hit in the research arena with the following story published in The Institute of HeartMath's Spring 2004 newsletter[8] "High school student David Merrell examined the effects of music on mice running through a maze. Would they learn to navigate faster with a specific kind of music? Before the mice began their listening regimen, David ran each of them through the maze to establish a base time of about 10 minutes. Then he started piping in the music.

For ten hours a day, one group heard classical and a second group heard hard rock. A third group heard no music at all. David put each mouse through the maze three times a week for three weeks. At the end of that time, the mice that had heard no music had managed to cut their time in half, averaging five minutes to complete the maze, simply as a result of regular practice. The mice that had listened to Mozart averaged an impressive one and a half minutes. For the mice that had listened to hard rock, navigating the maze had become more difficult and their original average time tripled to a staggering 30 minutes! Also worthy of note is the fact that David had tried to conduct a similar experiment the previous year, but cut it short when the hard rock mice killed each other off. "

Harvard University's Institute of Music and Brain Science is also conducting research on music's ability to affect the body. (See Chapter 9, ICU/CCU)

Super Learning

Many other informal studies continue to point to the usefulness of Baroque and Mozart's music to heighten abstract reasoning, comprehension, retention, and performance. For decades, researchers in Bulgaria have been using baroque music in their learning research. Headed by Dr. Lazimov[9], the studies find that Baroque music with high pitches and 60 beats per minute tempo has the greatest effect in energizing the brain which in turn increases learning. The music of that period (see Appendix E for a further description) creates a relaxed state that lowers blood pressure, synchronizes heartbeat and brain waves to slower, more efficient rhythms, and promotes hemisphericity, the synchronization of the right and left hemispheres. In this country, Ostrander and Schroeder have incorporated these findings into a program called Super Learning [7]. Using rhythm, breathing, and music, they have found learning accelerates, memory expands, and all is done in a fun atmosphere. CDs for use in the classroom cover arithmetic, vocabulary, math, languages, and provide background music for use during any cognitive activity. (See www.SuperLearning.com)

Hemisphere Synchronization

The two hemispheres of the brain, right and left, perform different functions for us. The qualities of the left hemisphere are rational, logical, linear, analytical, and organized, and some of its tasks include speech production and math calculation. The qualities of the right hemisphere are holistic rather than analytical; it is intuitive and metaphoric, and is involved in aesthetic perception, recognizing patterns, and emotions.

Left Hemisphere	Right Hemisphere
Logical	Creative
Analytical	Synthesizing
Mathematical	Artistic
Technical	Holistic
Problem Solving	Conceptualizing
Controlled	Interpersonal
Conservative	Emotional
Planning	Musical
Organizational	Spiritual
Administrative	Verbal
Sequential	Expressive
Procedural	Experiential

While the left hemisphere sorts through incoming information in a reductive manner, i.e., systematically considers every variable to find the best answer, the right hemisphere synthesizes information received--it arranges elements into a complete whole.

Many people develop one side of the brain to a greater degree than the other; this is known as 'straight dominance'. A left dominant person is a linear thinker, good with words but not much involved with the substance behind the words. Such people are good with specifics, remembering names, and critical thinking. People with a left brain dominance make good engineers, computer programmers, medical doctors, lawyers, critics, administrators, bookkeepers, and planners. Right brain dominant people are typically vague, diffuse, poetic, intuitive, good in aesthetic matters, but they have difficulty in getting down to specifics or in 'putting two and two together'. These people make good artists, psychologists, philosophers, writers, musicians, social workers, and policy makers. Although it is obvious that neither extreme is desirable, our society has been geared toward developing left hemisphere abilities, neglecting important right hemisphere operations. These are the first subjects 'to go' in school budget cuts: music, art, physical education, and audio-visual supplies. According to the cutter, the reason 'Johnny can't read' or do his math is that not enough emphasis is put on 'the basics' --left brain activities. In fact, the situation is just the opposite: not enough stimulation of the synthesizing, experiencing, poetic side--the right hemisphere. This is the part of the brain that is naturally used in the creative arts. Teachers and researchers keep reporting that kids learn better and faster when they: 1) experience what they are learning; 2) are having fun; and 3) have as many of their senses stimulated as possible.

Estimates vary, but there is agreement among brain researchers that humans use only a small portion of their mental capacity--from 10-13%. The obvious question arising from this observation and the known facts about holistic learning is: how can we tap some, or all, of that unused potential?

Hemi-Sync

Exploring the concept of hemisphericity by applying scientific brain-wave theories, the late Robert Monroe patented a synthesizer that brings the brain's hemisphere into synchronization. (This process is described in detail in Chapter 7). This system is based on the discovery that optimal learning takes place when the individual is in a certain state of consciousness, when the brain waves being generated are at a particular frequency. This optimal learning state has been established as the theta state, when the brain waves are cycling at 4-7 Hz. and when combined with Hemi-Sync signals, learning takes place quickly and easily. (See more at www.MonroeInstutite.org.) Reports from the Monroe Institute indicate a significant increase in learning and right brain attributes of cooperation, happiness, and general well-being. There are several CDs designed specifically to assist learning that contain these signals. (See Appendix A).

Recommendations for Music Assisted Learning

From the above cited research and other sources, it is clear that to use music successfully while studying, concentrating, and learning, certain conditions must be maintained. While doing cognitive work, each of the elements described in Chapter 1 must have particular characteristics.

Beat - Use music of 60-72 bpm
Rhythm - music should have simple, unchanging rhythm
Melody - strong, simple melody
Harmony - simple and unchanging
Timbre - strings, flute, piano, solo instruments with orchestra

The Baroque era in music contains a wealth of music that is suitable for this. Also good is the music of Mozart (second movements of concertos), Handel, Corelli, and others as listed in Appendix A under Cognitive Work. The Lind Institute has two CDs: *Classical Harmonies** and *Classical Melodies,* that incorporate all the appropriate elements. There are several Hemi-sync CDs that are also specifically programmed for learning: *Remembrance, Baroque Gardens, and Concentration* work well*.

ADD/ADHD

ADD/ADHD is defined as distractibility, impulsiveness, inattentiveness, absentmindedness, intrusiveness, talkativeness, and restlessness. There are many factors contributing to these symptoms including inadequate diets, toxins, thyroid disorders, nutritional deficiencies and allergies. It would be very beneficial to begin eliminating all wheat, sugar, dairy, and red and blue dyes from the diet of those with ADD/ADHD. Wearing orange tinted glasses makes focus and concentration easier when reading.

An *ADD/ADHD** CD has been programmed with frequencies (tones) that are beneficial for all children but especially for those who have been diagnosed, whether on medication or not. Listening to these tones will begin to heal damage from medication and will increase the concentration levels of adults and children. The Hemi-sync CD

Remembrance* is an extremely interesting CD to use with this population. All of the teachers who have followed my recommendation to play this in their classrooms have reported back to me that the children almost immediately became settled, at least less restless, and able to focus in on their work. One teacher reported that in subsequent days if she forgot to play the CD, the students would either ask her to or put it on themselves. Barry Osser's *'So' Chord**, also containing hemi-sync signals, is also a good background CD as it provides a beautiful supportive sound for classrooms, home, and anywhere a calm and focused environment is desired.

Autism

The number of children with autism has grown substantially in the last 50 years. Autism has been associated with toxins, vaccines, and heredity. There appears to be a breakdown of the patterning in some of the chromosomes.

The *Autism** CD, containing frequencies (tones, not music), has been programmed to stimulate the brain at the subatomic level which may lead to greater awareness and coping abilities. The tones will also assist in relaxing muscles, balancing the hemispheres, and releasing tension. Individuals may be able to express themselves better and evolve with appropriate external stimulation after repeated listenings.

Also recommended are two Hemi-sync CDs: *Remembrance** and *'So' Chord.*

* Available from www.InnerHarmonyHealthCenter.com

[1]Kenny, C.B. *The Myth Artery: The Magic of Music Therapy.* Atascadero, CA: Ridgeview Publishing Co. 1982.

[2]Hevner, K. "The Affective Characteristics of certain Elements of Musical Form." *Psychological Bulletin:*31, 678-679. 1934.

[3]Gatewood, Esther. "An Experimental study of the Nature of Musical Enjoyment." in Schoen, Max (ed*).* *The Effects of Music.* N.Y.:Harcourt, Brace & Co. , Inc. 1927.

[4]Altshuler, I. "Music as a Therapeutic Agent." in Schullian, D. and Schoen, M. (Eds). *Music and Medicine.* N.Y.: H.Schuman, Inc. 1948.

[5]Shatin, l. "Alteration of Mood via Music." *Journal of Psychology:* 75, 81-86. 1970.

[6]Shallcross, Doris. *Teaching Creative Behavior.* 1984.

[7]Weinberger, N.M. The 'Mozart Effect': A Small Part of the Big Picture". *MuSICA Research Notes:* Vol. VII, 11, Winter 2000.

[8]Instutite of HeartMath , www.Heartmath.com

[9]Ostrander & Schroeder. *SuperLearning* 2000

CHAPTER 4

USES OF MUSIC IN PSYCHOLOGY

I am Music, who with soft tones
Knows how to quiet each troubled heart
And now with noble anger or with love
Can ignite the most frozen minds.

I with my golden lyre sing so
That mortal ears are charmed thereby
And thus to the sonorous harmony
Of Heaven's Lyre I entice the soul.
Preface to the opera "Orpheus" by Monteverdi as sung by the Spirit of Music

Twentieth century psychiatry was dominated by Freudian psychoanalytic theory, which is concerned with an individually oriented view of inner conflict. Psychoanalysis is a verbal process that consists of uncovering repressed traumatic material. The mind is perceived as the source of change, and the body is but a means of implementation; thus a Cartesian split between mind and body is encouraged. Practitioners of psychoanalysis tend to emphasize and encourage verbal therapies even though there is research to show that this type of psychotherapy is appropriate for only a small percentage of the population[1.] In using Freudian terms to describe how music works in an individual, music therapist Lawrence Walters postulates that the id, ego, and superego admit music freely and allow it to integrate and reconcile all three aspects of personality. The listener then receives through the music a symbolic experience that bypasses the intellect. It makes connection with psychological processes within and transforms it into a healing process. Psychodynamically oriented music therapy depends on an understanding of psychodynamics that emphasizes three areas: 1) the sequential development of the personality; 2) the role of the unconscious; and 3) the transference of patient feelings for others onto the therapist.

However, transference is not regarded as the only operative relationship in this therapy. The therapist becomes an active supporter who helps the patient to learn, to mature, and to grow emotionally by working through problems on a more realistic level. A survey of the literature reveals that most therapists with this philosophy who work with music are professionally trained psychologists who have experienced the effects of music and now incorporate it into their practice.

INITIAL INTERVIEW

The first session with a psychologist or psychiatrist is usually an anxious experience for the client. Depending upon the type of music selected, when it is played in the background during these initial sessions, there will be a definite effect upon the patient. Soothing music promotes more interaction and affect-responses, as it assists in calming anxieties and defenses. Stimulating music and no music do not change the high level of anxiety.

TREATMENT PROCEDURES

Within the therapy session itself, therapists use music in a variety of creative ways with individuals and groups.

Musical Prescriptions

The traditional mode of incorporating music into a session was an outgrowth of psychotherapy in mental hospitals. The psychotherapists realized the connection between mind and body, and prescribed musical pieces for such conditions as high blood pressure connected with emotions, anger, depression, anxiety, and emotional fatigue.[2] Like the ancient Greeks, each therapist has evolved precise musical prescriptions for individual patients which take into account the underlying character of both disease and music. Recent research emphasizes the use of music in conjunction with other sensory modalities such as color, light, and tactile stimulation. Increased responses are observed when these modalities are paired with music.

Psychodrama

Psychodrama is a technique of 'acting out' feelings substituting the therapist or others in a group situation for significant people in the client's life. One therapist, Joseph Moreno, incorporates an ensemble of six to eight musicians who improvise around the emotional attitude of the client to facilitate awareness of repressed feelings. The feelings can then be acknowledged, externalized, and processed for insights. Since most therapists do not have at their disposable a group of musicians, using recorded music to enhance a scenario would be most beneficial. The therapist should choose music that would elicit the underlying emotion so the client can feel and externalize it in the process of the psychodrama.

Singing

Many therapists have their clients vocalize during their sessions, i.e. the client actively participates through improvisatory singing or toning. When a client does this, there is an unconscious projecting of inner conflicts into the voice. These conflicts stem from the mother-child symbiotic formation and reveal themselves in one's voice. Asking the client to feel her voice, or project different feeling into the voice can be a source for examination and discussion. Also, recording the session and having the client play it back between sessions can be a further reservoir for insight.

Emphasizing humor and enjoyment is another approach. Therapists have groups of clients do vocal exercises to express sounds and feelings. They progress to singing, jam sessions, musical performances and programs. The results include increased communication, resocialization, and ego strengthening.

Toning is an approach based upon singing a single tone, which can vary in pitch. It assists in reorganizing body cells that are out of alignment and therefore causing physical distress. It is the vibration established by the singing that assists in vibrating the cells back into normal patterns. A simultaneous effect occurs with feelings: a shaking up of the emotions and catharsis, followed by a feeling of well-being. In his work with toning, Don Campbell[3] finds a correlation between the quality and range of tones an individual produces and emotional blockages. Campbell's process frees the emotions by guiding the client in singing new sounds, working with the breath, and expanding vocal capabilities.

Sound Dialogues

Similar to mirroring, this exercise calls for members in a group to explore making sounds and dialogue with each other using instruments. Discussion centers on how they perceive and respond to the sound, both emotionally and intellectually. This process invariably develops insight into how their feelings and past experiences are projected into what they hear. The process also helps individuals to become more aware of listening patterns and the use of other sensory modalities. In my own practice I have found this technique very useful with couples. Using small drums, each takes a turn beating out a pattern and having the other repeat it back. It is always amazing to them how inaccurate they are in their 'echo'. This directly relates to their inability to listen carefully and to be able to repeat back what they heard their partner say.

Lyric Writing/Discussion

How one relates to lyrics can also be a revelation of unconscious aspects of the maternal relationship. The content of the song is interpreted as an expression of dominant transference or a defense issue. Psychotherapist Tom Ficken[4] has his patients rewrite songs, adding verses or substituting words. He also plays recorded songs that relate to the patient's problems. Clients have also been requested to find songs or music that would tell their group therapy peers more about themselves. Through this non-threatening modality a person is then able to share more of himself with a group and to invite the group to experience these threatening emotions together. This helps validate and defuse the negative feelings and stimulate healing ones. Some of the songs that I have found to be particularly useful include:

The Boxer	Simon & Garfunkle
Bridge Over Troubled Water	Simon & Garfunkle
Flowers Are Red	Harry Chapin
I Am a Rock	Simon & Garfunkle
Is That All There Is	Peggy Lee
It Was a Very Good Year	Frank Sinatra
Let the Sunshine In	from "Hair"
Prisoner in Disguise	Linda Ronstadt
The Rose	Bette Midler
Tradition	from "Fiddler on the Roof"
To Dream the Impossible Dream	from 'Man of LaMancha'
You've Got a Friend	James Taylor

Other techniques are to ask participants in a group to write stories or draw to music, to discuss lyrics in relation to themselves, and also to put music to slides or magazine pictures. Through these music related activities, group members learn more about themselves and improve their social and communications skills.

Paint to Music

This has been the subject of much controversy between art and music therapists. Some art therapists believe music to be too directive, while music specialists contend the music moves into the subconscious more quickly than unassisted attempts to facilitate the expression of psychological material. Researchers have found all subjects are affected by music while painting. They have also found that the pattern and mood of the music are reflected in the paintings, i.e. distress, conflict, catastrophe were themes in pictures painted to stimulating music and more pastoral scenes were painted in response to sedative music. Other correlations were also noted between the choice of music and the amount of color and movement in the paints, and in the degree of attention and concentration the patient exhibited.

Robert Cooke[5], a child psychologist, has applied these findings to his work with children and play therapy. Playing music helped to calm hyperactive children, to open communication and establish rapport, increase the attention to the artwork and to free deeper emotions. The artwork was not analyzed according to psychoanalytic theory, but the music and art provided discussion by the children. Although predominantly popular songs were used, the most provocative art and discussions were stimulated by classical music.

Imagery

The use of classical music to stimulate imagery in a therapy session was developed by music therapist Helen Bonny[6]. Her Guided Imagery and Music (GIM) technique is roughly based on the Psychosynthesis model of Roberto Assiagioli and archetypes identified by Carl Jung. It involves the 'lower unconscious, the unconscious, ordinary consciousness, and the transpersonal (for a more detailed discussion see Chapter 3). The process consists of expanding awareness of the self into both higher and deeper levels of consciousness. This is accomplished through music's ability to bypass the ego, touch the subconscious levels, and stimulate imagery. Listening in a relaxed state to specifically programmed CDs of classical music, the client freely verbalizes the ongoing imagery to the therapist. This metaphoric imagery is later discussed and related to the person's daily life. The CDs are programmed in a similar manner to Altshuler's[7] strategy of 'level' attacks used with severely mentally ill populations. The music arouses the attention of the client, modifies her mood, and then stimulates imagery and associations. Calling up past experiences means bringing back to mind certain basic realities that act as a bridge between the patient's mind and the outer world. By repeating the music daily, the temporary effect that occurs in the therapist's office can be lengthened.

Helen Bonny also refers to music as a bridge, but in reverse: participants in a GIM session often are attempting to expand conscious awareness into subconscious and transpersonal realms, so in this context music is a bridge from ordinary reality to the subconscious. Like others previously mentioned who have researched music's ability to stimulate imagery, Bonny has found similarities of themes and images among listeners, supporting Jung's theories of archetypes. Often GIM sessions include self-expression through art. After listening to the CD, the client is asked to fill in a twelve-inch circle using pastels. This mandala reflects the consciousness of the person at the time of the exercise. Drawing on the theories and research of art therapist Joan Kellogg, the mandala is regarded as a mirror of the psyche at that given moment, and as an insight into what is about to unfold. Changes noted over a period of time in a series of mandalas can reveal growth or disintegration. This can be a meaningful tool for client and therapist.

DIAGNOSTIC USES OF MUSIC IN THERAPY
Music Preferences
There have also been attempts to use music as a means of diagnosis. The first and most common method focuses on finding correlations and distinctions between musical preferences of normal and disordered persons. Responses are of indirect value to psychotherapy, as some light has been thrown on the personalities of the subjects and on their unconscious attitudes and conflicts.

The Institute for Personality and Ability (IPAT) Music Preference Test is a standardized gauge in which subjects are requested to rate their preferences among a hundred musical excerpts. The choices are correlated to personality characteristics, giving the therapist a broader personality profile of the patient.

Projection Tests
The other major emphasis in diagnosis has been the issue of projection. Researchers have found normal persons and schizophrenics tell markedly different stories after having listened to a range of musical excerpts. All stories tended to be autobiographical and could reveal inner fantasies, illogical or disassociated thinking, and egocentricity. Reliability, or consistency, was high both in terms of matching subjects and the stories they tell, and in connecting story types and diagnostic categories.

Rolando Benezon[8], a sound researcher in South America, has developed a similar successful approach employing a series of familiar sounds. His three projective sound tests are each five minutes in length, and include a logical ordering of sounds such as: ticking clock, sound of alarm, yawning voice, filling a wash basin, voice saying 'NO', etc. Subjects are asked to write a story for each series of sounds, and to give it a title. Results of each test have been consistent with other projective tests.

Thematic Apperception Test (TAT)

A slightly different approach has been to provide background music to a traditionally non-music task in order to judge the effect. Using picture #9 from the TAT, two pieces of music of varying mood were played while subjects wrote stories. Picture #9 is two pictures: 1. four men in overalls lying on the grass; 2. a young woman with a magazine and purse in hand looking from behind a tree at a young woman in a party dress running along the beach. Results indicated that the choice of music had a significant effect on the content of the interpretations, which corresponded to the emotional content of the music. Interestingly, the quieter piece had the most effect: it reduced tension and produced more happiness, hope, and contentment in the story's content.

In our everyday lives music is used to direct our emotions as we watch TV or a movie. How different the effect would be if a waltz were played in the background when the great white shark in the movie "Jaws" was on the prowl!

MUSICAL PRODUCTION

To many critics, the major drawback in the use of music for diagnosis is the fact that virtually all of the techniques are verbal, and elicit patient *response* rather than patient *production.* It is argued that this reliance on response robs diagnosis of the spontaneity and authenticity found in art and advance/movement therapy diagnostic techniques. Music therapists Paul Nordoff and Clive Robbins[9], though, have developed an evaluation scale based on the child-therapist relationship during improvised musical activity and the degree of musical communicativeness.

Using improvised music to communicate with autistic and psychotic children, they engage the children in a co-creative process. The initial interaction establishes an activity relationship, then, the more the child reveals, the more the therapist can direct work toward sustained developmental contact. Improvised music is utilized to awaken responses at the 'normal' level of the child's fragmented, disorganized psyche. The playful give and take with the therapist leads to sharing and working together, and constitutes a completely new relationship for the child. This method, then, depends upon direct musical production, not verbal response.

Music Therapist Evelyn Heimlich[10] has adapted this technique in her work with disturbed children wherein imitation of their musical patterns leads to composition. Adding percussive sounds to made-up stories, singing songs appropriate to problem or mood, and pointing to music comprise her successful, eclectic approach to music therapy.

SUMMARY -USING MUSIC IN PSYCHOLOGICAL SETTINGS

Group Sessions:
>   Use of music alone: psychodrama, singing, toning, song
>   Discussion, circle drumming, sound dialogues
>   Music to stimulate artistic expression
>   Music to stimulate writing and lyric writing
>   Music and guided imagery

Individual Sessions:
>   During the initial interview
>   Guided Imagery & Music
>   Vibro Acoustics (see Chapter 7)
>   With biofeedback
>   Singing, toning, individual music making
>   As a projection test

As Adjunct
>   During meals to set a mood
>   During exercise to increase performance and participation
>   For entertainment
>   Modifying the general atmosphere (Chapter 3-Mood Alteration)

RECOMMENDATIONS

Below is a summary of the benefits of using music in a psychological setting along with some specific music suggestions that colleagues and myself have found to be useful.

<u>Decreasing:</u> (the 'So' Chord* is highly effective in all of these categories)

chaotic behavior	Concentration*, Remembrance*
anxiety/panic attacks	Deep Relax*, Meta music*
insomnia	surf sounds, Super Sleep*, Sound Sleeper*
respiratory problems	Metamusic*, Lung Repairs* Deep Relax*
loneliness	old favorites, Spirit Guide, The Visit*
pain	Pain Control
boredom	Masterworks*, The Visit Energy Walk* Spirit Guide*, old favorites
anger	Remembrance* (highly effective when combined with biofeedback)
substance abuse	Remembrance*, The Visit*, Deep Relax*, Blessings
internal tensions	Remembrance*, Deep Relax*, Blessings, Unity

<u>Increasing:</u>

communication, self expression, socialization
music with messages(love, loyalty, friendship, etc)

expression of emotions
music/songs that match the client's emotions

The appendix also has many music suggestions to assist with the above.

*Cds that contain Hemi-Sync signals. All cds recommended above can be purchased from www.InnerHarmonyHealthcenter.com

[1]Glass, G. and Kliegl, R. "An apology for Research Integration in the Study of Psychotherapy." *Journal of Consulting and Clinical Psychology:* 51, p.31. 1983.
[2]Podolsky, Edward. *Music Therapy.* N.Y.: Philosophical Library. 1954.
[3]Campbell, Don. *Music and Miracles.* Quest Books, Wheaton, IL. 1992.
[4]Ficken, T. "Use of Songwriting in a Psychological Setting." *Journal of Music Therapy:* 13(4), 163-172. 1976.
[5]Cooke, Robert. "The Use of Music I Play Therapy." *Journal of Music Therapy:* 6, P.66-75.1969.
[6]Bonny, Helen. *GIM Monographs I,II,III.* Port Townsend, WA.: ICM West. 1978.
[7]Altshuler, Ira. "Music as a Therapeutic Agent." in Schullian, D. and Schoen, M. (Eds) *Music and Medicine.* N.Y.: H. Schuman, Inc. 1948.
[8]Benezon, Rolando. *Music Therapy Manual.* Springfield, IL. Charles C. Thomas. 1981.
[9]Nordoff, Paul and Robbins,C. *Music Therapy in Special Education.* N.Y>: J. Day Co. 1971
   Nordoff and Robbins. *Creative Music Therapy.* N.Y.: J. Day Co. 1977.
[10]Heimlich, Evelyn. "The Specialized Use of Music as a Mode of Communication in the Treatment of Disturbed   Children. *Journal of American Academy of Child Psychiatry:* 4, p.86-122.1965

CHAPTER 5

EFFECTS OF MUSIC ON THE BODY

Every sickness is a musical problem.
The healing, therefore, is a musical resolution.
The shorter the resolution, the greater the musical talent of the doctor.
Novalis, 18th Century German Poet

The idea that music may be a key to healing the mind and body has fascinated western culture for millennia. There exist numerous accounts of the healing power of music from ancient Greece, where Apollo was the god of both music and medicine. In the healing temples, music was used not only to calm the soul, but also to induce ecstatic experiences to awaken the body's own curative powers. Pythagoras of Samos is credited with being the father of music therapy in the sixth century. His philosophy was based on the premise that the universe and all its creations are founded and governed by the laws of music and vibration. It encompassed music, healing, science, mathematics, medicine, and nutrition. He composed distinct songs and music for various ailments and believed that music contributes greatly to health and, if used in an appropriate manner, is capable of producing "the most beneficial correction of human manner and lives." (Iambilichus of Chalcis, 250-325 A.D.) His philosophy and teachings dominated the Mediterranean culture for 800 years.

Effects of Music on the Body

While most of us intuitively know that "Music hath charms to soothe the savage breast" (William Congreave), exactly how music makes its way into our thinking and why it affects our bodies is still being researched with new findings each year. The following is a summary of the current research:

~ Because music is nonverbal, it is able to move directly through the auditory cortex to the center of the limbic system, the midbrain network that governs most of our emotional experience as

51

well as basic metabolic responses such as body temperature, blood pressure, and heart rate.

~Music may be able to activate the flow of stored memory material across the corpus callosum, a collection of fibers connecting the left and right sides of the brain, helping the two to work in harmony.

~Music may be able to stimulate the production of endorphins, natural opiates secreted by the hypothalamus, which produce feelings akin to love and decreases pain.

~Sound is transformed into nervous influx in the inner ear, sent on to the brain cortex, and from there to the entire body, to tone up the whole system by increasing the electrical potential of the brain and thereby imparting greater dynamism to the whole body.

~Musically naïve persons have higher alpha brain waves (relaxed state) in the right hemisphere, and respond to music almost equally in both hemispheres during listening. In other words, different components of music are registered in different hemispheres, so that both the halves participate in its perception and analysis. Musicians, on the other hand, have higher alpha waves in the left hemisphere, and perceive melody and chords with the left hemisphere[1].

~Sound has been shown to trigger the production of certain chemicals in the brain:

> Serotonin which eases pain
> Acetycholine which is connected to intelligence
> Catecholamines which are vital for learning and memory
> DHEA which increases your resistance to disease
> Melatonin which aides sleep and therefore phsical body regeneration[2]

Of the several web sites that document research, the most useful is the large music therapy research database at the University of Texas at http://iucairss.utsa.edu. Check Appendix C for more sites.

Effects of Music Elements on the Body

Assuming a person is generally receptive to therapeutic music, the physiological effects most associated with treatment are in direct correlation to the specific characteristics of each musical selection. For example, a stirring Sousa march will affect bodily processes differently than a Brahms waltz. Thanks to modern technology and decades of research on this topic, the following conclusions, as shown in Table l, are accepted as valid.

		MUSIC'S EFFECTS ON THE BODY
RHYTHM	Strong -	pulse rate, blood pressure, circulation, pain ultradian cycles
	Even -	muscle recruitment, gait
	Simple -	brain wave functioning
TEMPO	Lively -	increases: metabolism, muscle energy, respiration, internal secretions, GSR, BP, heart rate
	Sedative-	decreases: metabolism, muscle energy, respiration, BP, heart rate stimulates pain relieving peptides affects pupil constriction
	60 bpm -	stabilizes brain and hearing
PITCH	High -	tension
	Low -	relaxation
VOLUME		Loud (over 130 db) - pain, then permanent damage with sustained listening
MELODY	Simple -	strengthens listening ability
TIMBRE	Calming -	cello, piano, harp, guitar, strings, flute
	Tension	harpsichord, violin

Table 1.

As we will see in the chapter on applying music in a medical setting, these factors must be considered when attempting to use music as a healing agent. The application of music then becomes prescriptive.

53

For example, one might take a common symptom like tension headaches and apply the above criteria for selecting a piece of music that would assist in decreasing the pain.

Beat/Pulse/Rhythm

This is the strongest component of music, the 'toe tapping' aspect. It is central to the music of primitive peoples, and although we consider our music to be more sophisticated and civilized, the overriding essence of popular music today is an incessant beat. The heart is the body's central rhythm, directly correlated to rhythm in music. It has been conclusively demonstrated that blood pressure, pulse rate, and circulation can be directly affected by strong rhythms in music. So what type of beat, pulse, and rhythm would be beneficial in reducing a headache that may also be pulsing? Choosing a simple straightforward beat and rhythm that are not the main focus in the piece would provide stability and ease of listening.

Tempo

The tempo or speed of the music appears to have multiple physiologic effects on the body. It has the ability to increase bodily metabolism, increase or decrease muscular energy, accelerate respiration and decrease its regularity, to influence internal secretions, and to affect galvanic skin response (electrical resistance of the skin). Most researchers agree that it is tempo that is the major cause of one's physiologic response to music. To ease a headache one would definitely want music that is steady and slower than heart rate, i.e. less than 60-72 beats per minute.

Melody

This is the humming or singing aspect of a piece of music, the tune. It appears to play an important part in strengthening the listening abilities and as background when one is performing cognitive work. It has been correlated with brain function. Choosing music with either a simple melody or even no melody would be best for the purpose of decreasing a headache.

Harmony

These are the extra notes in addition to the melody, the cushion of sonorities organized as chords that often support and enhance the melody. These note combinations can be either tonal or atonal, i.e., pleasing or less pleasing to uncomfortable. This perception does change with respect to mood and musical understanding. Harmony has been associated with the inner organic workings of the body: the pulmonary, circulatory, and digestive systems. Tonal music with no changes in key or complex harmonic patterns would assist in decreasing a headache.

Pitch

The highness or lowness of a sound acts upon the autonomic nervous system: high pitches create tension and low pitches facilitate relaxation. Our headache would most likely increase if we used music sung only by sopranos. We want to choose something that has an underpinning of low sounds.

Timbre

This refers to the quality of sound expressed by the instruments playing the music. In the work of Helene Corinne and Helen Bonny, these musical instruments have been observed to correlate with particular body parts:

> head.................flute, piano, harp
> nerves...............stringed instruments
> thorax...............cello
> bones............ .....brass instruments
> overall system.......organ

Depending upon the level of intensity of the headache, we might suggest some music played on the flute, harp, or full string orchestra.

Volume

Extreme listening volume demonstrably causes physical pain. College students who frequent discos or other venues where loud music is played have high frequency hearing loss. Musicians, too, suffer hearing loss if they play highly amplified music for long periods. No matter how beautiful a piece of music may be, if it is played loud enough to be painful, no one will want to listen to it. It goes without saying, then, your music will need to be played softly.

To summarize our selection: the music would be slow, have a steady simple rhythm and harmony, simple or no melody, be played on flute, harp, or string orchestra and contain mostly lower pitches.

Variables Affecting Success

The ability of music to enter one's system and be therapeutic depends upon a number of variables. The person's mental state and willingness to listen to the music and identify with it are just as important to consider as the music selection itself. You might choose the most appropriate music to reduce the headache but if the person won't listen to it, you will not have positive results.

Physiologic State Stated simply: how badly you feel physically determines how willing you are to listen to music. In extreme pain, for instance, most people will not even try music as an analgesic, but will usually choose a pain shot or pill, preferring the instant effect. However, once the pain has been dulled, patients will be more willing to try the power of music. This can become a learned effect, and later, when pain becomes sharper, music will be received more readily than medication. If you know that listening to a Bach chorale lessened your pain once you will be more likely to try it again and expect to experience the same effect. More discussion on this in Chapter 8.

Mental State Just as with the physical state, if a person is experiencing extreme emotions such as depression, grief, or anger, she may not be wholly receptive to music's charms. As discussed in the previous chapter, though, by playing music that matches the mood, then vectoring (moving) slowly to a more desired mood with music, one can experience a change and may then be more open to listening.

A chattering mind will also detract from one's experience with music. I often suggest to patients to put all of your cares, worries, and concerns in a bubble, see the bubble drift away and then turn on the music.

Willingness to Listen In order for music to be healing, a person needs to be willing to identify with it, and then to become involved with the sounds and patterns. It seems that the better you are at listening to music, the greater will be your gain. For this to be accomplished, the composer Roger Sessions[3] has outlined four states to becoming a good listener.

1. Come to the music with NO preconceived ideas and listen without effort. Follow the music as well as you can in its continuity. Try to identify with it. I ask clients to come to the music with an open mind, or with a childlike curiosity.

2. ENJOY simultaneously while hearing the music--let it communicate with you. Allow yourself the fun of being taken away by the sounds.

3. Strive for musical understanding. Take the music into your consciousness and remake it, or into your imagination for your own use: whistle, hum, think it to yourself, or condense the sounds to memory in patterns of sensations. For those of you who wish to begin to really learn about music and to appreciate it:

Cultivate your senses: be aware of rhythm, articulation, contrast, and accent.

Follow just the bass line movement, not just the melody.

Do repeated listening to become familiar and friendly with a selection. This is great to do on car commutes.

4. Be discriminating. Become a critic with LOVE. Learn to differentiate between lasting and fleeting impressions, satisfying and semi-satisfying experiences, and your own impressions. Learn to cultivate a sense of values: music is unequal in quality, as evidenced by differences in life spans of works. These pieces drop out of public interest for a reason.

Listening must be preceded then by mental and physical adjustments which that facilitate and condition subsequent responses to music. There are also other personal adjustments that need to be considered that are products of a person's life.

Personal Preference This is an important consideration in many cases, although the research from ScientificMusicTherapy.com suggests something different (see paragraph below).

The preference for vocal or instrumental music was a very important aspect of Helen Bonny's prepared tapes for surgery. She and I both found that people had definite likes for one or the other.

One's socioeconomic and cultural background often makes a difference. A person of first generation non-European culture quite possibly will not be willing to listen to a Beethoven sonata or Montavani orchestra, no matter now innately healing the music is.

And the Type A personality sometimes has difficulty listening to anything that is not directly related to her profession, goal or high energy.

The Effect of Intent

One of the most interesting realizations from all of my years in psychology and sound healing is the effect between a person's intent and the outcome. The listener's beliefs about the aesthetic experience in general and musical experience in particular will affect the outcome. Does she believe music to be beneficial, beautiful, or just another aspect of life? I remember approaching a middle-aged man waiting for knee surgery. I asked him if he would like to be a part of my doctoral study and listen to some music before and after surgery. His response, "I hate music," stunned me. This is something I can't imagine, that there isn't one piece of music that wouldn't touch him in a satisfying way. I often wish I had been able to talk with him further.

Some people also believe that only modern medicine and medications will be helpful for their condition. For these folks, I give a very short background on the many uses of music as a healing agent and ask them to try it anyway, as it will at least be pleasant. Most who try it are surprised at the positive outcomes. Time after time I have seen patients either have an amazing outcome from listening to a CD, or little to nothing at all. As I explored with them their initial thoughts and beliefs about using the CD, I found that those persons who had the belief that the CD was going to be helpful, or at least they were open to trying the experience, had the most positive outcomes. One way to look at it is this is just another example that there is a connection between the mind and the body. From a quantum physics perspective, it is known that in our subatomic levels the emotions directly affect the actions of the biochemical.

HeartMath Biofeedback is a dramatic visual of this effect. Those persons who just 'think' about love, sincere appreciation, joy, etc. show no effect on their physiology! Just as soon as you really *feel* the emotions, the monitors change and there is a positive connection between the head and the heart that effects the entire mind/body/spirit/emotional field.

So, the intent of the patient influences their experience, as does the intent of the performers on the CD, and the healthcare practitioner who administers the CD. It is very important to align all of this. You many not be aware of the intent of the performers, but you can certainly monitor your own.

Scientific Music Therapy

An interesting series of CDs is currently being composed by Peter Hubner in Holland. Medical Resonance Therapy Music® consists of a number of medical music preparations created in international cooperation with Hubner *and* physicians. The project is based on the works of Pathagoras, the famous early European physician, musician, and mathematician and many great scientists and thinkers who followed him. Their mutual interest was in researching nature's laws of harmony in a purposeful scientific manner, and utilizing them for medicine and health. It is based on three decades of intensive research and developments. It has been objectively examined and clinically applied at universities, research institutions and clinics throughout Europe, Israel, and Russia.

The preparations (CDs) have proven to be 4-8 times as effective for the release of psycho-physiological manifestations of stress as a pharmaceutical preparation. For this reason, it is the only Medical Music Preparation approved by the Government in Germany and is available in 22,000 German Pharmacies. It is covered completely by their insurance programs.

One of their interesting research results was the noticeable effect of the listener's mindset on the effect on their body. When a group was just given the CD and told to listen to it, @40% of them had no effect on their physiology and said that not only did they not like the music, but would not want to listen any more. Then the group was told that the music *was not* composed for entertainment, but was created purely for medical purposes. The subsequent listening experience produced a greater percentage of positive effects! More information on these remarkable CDs is at:www.scientificmusictherapy.com. CDs can be ordered from www.InnerHarmonyHealthCenter.com

Effect of Music on the Body's Electromagnetic Field (EMF)

Music is a complex series of sound vibrations created by the motion of air molecules. When these vibrations or waves reach the ear, an amazing process occurs compressing these waves to fit smaller and smaller spaces. This process increased the pressure of sound 150-200 times. The sound is translated into electrical impulses, which are conveyed to the processing center. But the waves of sound are not merely funneled into the ears; they reach the entire body surface, and this is highly porous. (Heat, air, sweat are released through these pores) People are constantly being bombarded by sound waves in daily life. What effect this has is only partially known. However, current research is attempting to evaluate the effect sound has on the EMF that surrounds one's body. This essential vibrational field is common to all living organisms, extending beyond the solid body for anywhere from two inches to as much as eight feet. Another term for this radiant effect is the aura; there are people who are able to see this field. Kirilian photography is a static-electrical technology allowing the rest of us to view these fields. Valerie Hunt, professor emeritus at UCLA, has spent her entire career validating this phenomenon, and has devised a computer-assisted video technique to film a person's field. Through these techniques, and by aura-sensitive persons, the field has been described as fluid, colorful, and ever changing. These characteristics appear to be influenced by the food we eat, strong electromagnetic fields, thoughts, and emotions. Listening to music appears to also have an effect on this field, depending upon the type of music and the person's receptivity. For example, listening to a piece of music subjectively experienced as "beautiful" extends and smoothes the field. The work of Valerie Hunt, Stanley Krippner, Peter Guy Manners, Christopher Hill, as well as the philosophy of Hindu medicine, all claim that the EMF is both a representation of the current physical/mental health AND a physical zone of influence in which to begin a healing process. Hunt[4] has demonstrated that externally changing the field of a patient who has a physical illness by applying a "healer's positive energy" results in the beginning stages of healing in the dis-eased area of the body. It is interesting to note, though, that physical healing will stop and reverse if emotional conflicts/issues are not examined and released. In other words, the emotional field appears to govern the physical.

Music/Sound and Imagery

As has been discussed in Chapters 3 & 4, imagery is capable of changing emotions and of revealing inner processes. Imagery can also affect a range of bodily functions including heart rate, perspiration, and blood pressure. When researchers have used the positron emission tomography (PET) scan to monitor the brain during imagery exercises, they have found that the same parts of the cerebral cortex are activated whether people imagine something or actually experience it. This suggests that vivid imagery can send a message from the cerebral cortex to the lower brain centers, including the emotional center, endocrine system and autonomic nervous system, which can then affect a range of bodily functions.

The relationship between music, imagery, and relaxation appears to be an especially potent one. In studies where music and imagery are monitored separately, they each are effective in reducing the stress symptoms. However, recent studies find that it is even more effective to pair music and imagery: the combination produced a greater relaxation response AND in those studies monitoring immune response, the level of IgA secreted was higher. A caveat must follow: **the selection of music, wording of the imagery exercises, and intent of the narrator is crucial.** These elements are just as important to consider as which medications to prescribe for a particular symptom. The imagery CDs carried by Inner Harmony have been programmed by imagery and music specialists and are highly recommended. (www.InnerHarmonyHealthCenter.com)

Studies Demonstrating No Effect

There are a number of studies that found no positive correlations between music and the monitored desired effect. It is the conclusion of researchers and validated by my own experience that most studies of this type appear to have the following characteristics in common:

~too short a listening time: times need to be longer than 20 minutes, or repeated 2-3x/day
~use of older, less sensitive monitoring devices
~statistically too small of a sample
~limited musical selection
~researchers were untrained in music therapy or music medicine
~no consideration of mental, physical, or cultural variables

To be effective, listening to music must be preceded by mental and physical adjustments that will facilitate and condition the subsequent responses to music. For music to have its fully desired effect, the listening time must be long enough to overcome counter-productive variables present and to engage the mind and emotions of the listener. The music administrator must account for the level of receptivity of the subject and the prevailing physical, emotional, and cultural conditions. In this way, the listener will be freed to engage with the music and become receptive to its "charms that soothe the savage breast".

---

[1]McElwain, J. Jaunita. "The Effect of Spontaneous and Analyzed Listening on the Evoked Cortical Action in the Left and Right Hemispheres of Musicians and Non-Musicans." *Journal of Music Therapy:* 16(4), pp. 180-189. 1979.
[2]www.neuroacoustic.com
[3]Sessions, Roger. *The Musical Experience of Composer, Performer, Listener.* Princeton, N.J.: Princeton University Press.1950.
[4]Hunt, Valerie. *Infinite Mind.* Malibu, CA: Malibu Publishing Co. 1996.

CHAPTER 6

MUSIC FOR THE SOUL

*Music is the bridge between
our daily lives and our higher self*
Suzanne Jonas, Ed.D. Sound Therapist

Not all music, or organized sounds, promotes healing. We all have experienced listening to pieces of music that we found painful, disgusting, or irritating. Just recall some of the music you may have heard on some radio stations, or booming from a teenager's car. Some music touches only our bodies, like music with hard, driving beats and rhythms, such as some rock music. The physiological effect is one of changing the heart rate (for further explanation see Chapter 5). Other music makes a greater impression on our minds. Music from the Baroque period (1600-1750) tends to do this. The predominant attribute of baroque music is melody with little variety in tempo, timbre, rhythm, or volume. Because the music tends to be logical, linear, and even, it induces the mind to imitate the same evenness. Music that we respond to emotionally is affecting our moods (see Chapter 3). Think of pieces of music that bring tears or joy or feelings of pride and majesty. But it is the music that affects all four aspects of ourselves that has the most healing effect, for we cannot separate out the parts of ourselves. Music that heals must touch all parts of our selves: our minds, bodies, emotions, and most importantly, our spirits. For instance, if you have a headache or indigestion, you probably will not want to do any mind work and you will most likely feel "down," Similarly, if you are depressed, you will have difficulty keeping your attention on your work, you may have interrupted sleep and appetite patterns, experience fatigue, and not care about things. You probably won't feel like hearing lively music and exercising. As composer Peter Hubner stated: *No healing can take place without addressing the soul.*

Finding music that touches our spirit-selves along with the other three aspects is difficult. In my experience and that of other researchers and practitioners, it is music of the great classical composers that contains the greatest opportunity for healing.

(However, I must admit that recently I have been having to adjust my thinking as I have been introduced to a few contemporary non-classical pieces of very effective 'soul' music.) Great music is the most many-sided: it is capable of presenting different dimensions to different generations, and it is capable of retaining its vitality through a variety of interpretations.

Albert Schweitzer said: "All true and deeply felt music, whether sacred or profane, journeys to heights where religion can always meet."

How do you discern between music that 'turns you on', is highly erotic or loving, and soul music?

The good is one thing; the sensuously pleasant another. These two, differing in their ends, both prompt to action. Blessed are they that choose the good; they that choose the sensuously pleasant miss the goal.

Both the good and the pleasant present themselves to men. The wise, having examined both, distinguish the one from the other. The wise prefer the good to the pleasant; the foolish, driven by fleshly desires, prefer the pleasant to the good. Katha Upanisha

Simply put, when you listen to 'soul music', it catches your attention, holds it, and moves you out of everyday thoughts and feelings. You may have strong sensory reactions: visual images, tingling in your body, energy rushes or warmth. You may feel as if your heart expands, be brought to tears, or receive instant 'knowings'. When you have finished listening, the music will leave you in a much different state than when you began. I remember the first time I heard Samuel Barber's *Adagio for Strings*. This is a lush piece for only the string sections of an orchestra. It starts quietly and builds to an incredible peak, which is sustained. As I began to hear the music I immediately became focused into the music, my surroundings fell away. Gradually I began to feel tinglings that increased into intense surges of energy. It was as if I had a dimmer switch attached to my electro-magnetic body and it was slowly being increased. By the time the peak came in the music I WAS the music. I can feel the same energy now as I write about it, though somewhat diminished. I'm sure if someone who could see auras had seen me then I would have been like a 1000 watt bulb! It took hours for the feelings to subside, during which time I felt such incredible peace and oneness with the Divine. The feelings, then, are not sexual/sensual, but a higher vibration.

In an attempt to study neural mechanisms underlying intensely pleasant emotional responses to music, Dr. Zatorre presents a study investigating "musical chills" response using positron emission tomography (PET)[1]. In the investigation, cerebral blood flow changes were measured in response to subject-selected music that elicited highly pleasurable experiences of "chills". Subjective reports of chills were accompanied by changes in heart rate, electromyogram, and respiration. As intensity of these chills increased, cerebral blood flow increases were observed in the ventral striatum (nucleus accumbance, in particular), the midbrain, and the orbitofrontal cortex, while its decreases were observed in the amygdula and the ventral medial prefrontal cortex. This suggests two possible systems that may be involved in emotional response to music. The brain regions comprising these two systems, activated or deactivated, are thought to be involved in reward and motivation, emotion and arousal. These brain structures are also known to be active in response to other euphoria-inducing stimuli, such as food, sex, and drugs and abuse. This finding links music with biologically relevant, survival-related stimuli via their common recruitment of brain circuitry involved in pleasure and reward.

Dr. Zatorre points to the fact that ancient reward/ motivation systems are present in musical emotional response, despite the fact that music has no direct biological survival value, based on which he also shares an interesting speculation on the evolutionary link between phylogenically older, survival-related brain systems and newer more cognitive systems. He suggests that music may possibly represent a special interaction between emotion and cognition.

These "energy rushes" can also be felt without musical stimulation when I am particularly "touched" by words and sights. I have discovered that they are my body's way of signaling when I am in touch with my soulself and am receiving more energy. Perhaps you, too, have felt these as tingling, shivers, or goose bumps during poetry, songs, or music, or hearing about wondrous ways human beings have connected with one another, or when in a particularly glorious setting. During those times your mind/body/emotions are in direct connection with your higher self and are then open to receiving more life energy from your soul. Kurt Leland, in his book *Music and the Soul*, calls these experiences Transcendental Musical Experiences, or TME's.

There are several pieces of music listed in the appendix under "Soul Music" that you might like to try in order to elicit a TME.

Soul Music Origins

Music that has the ability to touch your soul involved the composer in the same way. She did not write that piece of music simply for profit, but from a strong inner desire to express something larger than her. The psychologist Carl Jung[2] said there are two kinds of artists: the cerebral or psychological, and the impulsive or visionary. The cerebral composer draws from the conscious mind, or normal waking state. Her compositions reflect characteristics of her own psyche and/or those of her time period.

The visionary composer draws material from the subconscious or collective unconscious (see Chapter 4). When drawing from this reservoir the composer does not have free will; she allows the art to realize its purposes through her. It can, in effect, drain her of her humanity, and set her apart from society. Many of the great composers have led lonely lives in poverty and been misunderstood by their families and friends, not to mention their community. The visionary artist is deeply aware of the basic elements of music and is a master of her art, but she combines it with her imagination in a masterful way. Great artists transcend the human experience, and their music always points the human heart upward.

In Western classical music tradition prior to the twentieth century, serious music was usually the product of religious or spiritual ideals. Throughout the Middle Ages, the Catholic Church was the primary producer of serious music, all of which was intended for the glorification of God. In later centuries, even those works which were not overtly religious in nature were "nevertheless the creation of individuals whose very goal in life was solely and uncompromisingly to radiate throughout the world, by their art, the ideals of spirituality, joy, and brotherhood." (David Tame[3]) The music of such composers as Bach, Beethoven, Brahms, Handel, Mozart, and Wagner, for example, continue in popularity because of these qualities that touch our souls. Several great master composers have described their process as tapping into something greater than themselves.

I am convinced that there are universal currents of Divine Thought vibrating the ether everywhere and that anyone who can feel these vibrations is inspired provided he is conscious of the process and

66

possesses the knowledge and skill to present them...I have very definite impressions while in the trance-like state which is the prerequisite of all true creative effort. I feel that I am one with the vibrating Force, that it is omniscient, and that I can draw upon it to an extent that is limited only by my own capacity to do so...One supreme fact which I have discovered is that it is not will power but fantasy imagination that creates...Imagination is the creative force...imagination creates the reality. Richard Wagner

(My musical ideas) flow best and most abundantly when I cannot sleep, after a good meal, traveling in a carriage, or walking. Whence and how they come, I know not; nor can I force them...I do not hear in my imagination the parts successively, but I hear them all at once...All this inventing, this producing, takes place in a pleasing lively dream... I have my Divine Maker to thank for. But why my productions take from my hand that particular form and style that makes them Mozartish, and different from the works of other composers, is probably owning to the same cause which renders my nose so large or so aquiline, or, in short, makes it Mozart's, and different from those of other people. For I really do not study or aim at any originality.
Wolfgang Amadeus Mozart

Mozart was a prodigy and a genius. He stood 5'4", was unattractive, abusive, temperamental, irresponsible, and crass. But he wrote music that moved people then and now. His description of his composing process shows that he was an inspired artist and his music reflects much more than his personality. From a compositional standpoint "Mozart is just God's way of making the rest of us feel insignificant. Whenever you have just composed a piece of music you think is particularly good, it is humbling to think that Mozart probably wrote a better one when he was 9!" (D. Barber, music historian)

Several esoteric and metaphysical writers believe Mozart to be the purest of the composers so far on our planet. They describe his music to be full of the Divine light and have the ability to resonate with all peoples and cultures. He clearly loved to compose, could do it 'on the spot', and was brilliantly original. We use his music to assist in cognitive work, to delight, to relax, and to join with our spirit. One of his most sublime works, *Laudate Dominum,* will leave you in heaven!

To realize that we are one with the Creator as Beethoven did is a wonderful and awe-inspiring experience. Very few human beings ever come to that realization, and that is why there are so few great composers or creative geniuses...I always contemplate all this before commencing to compose. This is the first step. When I feel vibrations which thrill my whole being. In this exalted state I see clearly what is obscure in my ordinary moods; then I feel capable of drawing inspiration from above as Beethoven did...Those vibrations assume the form of distinct mental images...Straight away the ideas flow in upon me, directly from God, and not only do I see distinct themes in the mind's eye, but they are clothed in the right forms, harmonies, and orchestration. Measure by measure the finished product is revealed to me when I am in those rare, inspired moods...I have to be in a semi-trance condition to get such results--condition when the conscious mind is in temporary abeyance, and the subconscious is in control, for it is through the subconscious mind, which is a part of Omnipotence, that the inspiration comes. Johannes Brahms

After 1900 a new breed of musicians appeared who did not share the same motives as many of their predecessors. Whereas the great composers of the past had composed for the sublime, the new generation expressed more the emotional, physical, and mental levels. In the past when composers had experimented with new techniques, it had been to improve their music. For the most part, twentieth century composers created music for the sake of experimenting with new sounds (Debussy), realism (Mussorgsky), intellectualism (Schoenberg, Webern, Berg), unemotionalism (Ives), physicality (Stravinsky), existentialism (Varese, Cage), relaxation (Halpern, New Age Music), and repetition (Glass, minimalists). That is not to say that any composer could not compose a piece of 'soul' music, or that every piece of music Brahms composed is spirit inspired. An absolutely little jewel of a piece is R. Strauss' *Breit Uber Mein Haupt*, though he is not particularly thought of as a 'soul' composer. Kurt Leland gives an excellent explanation of these types of composers in his book *Music and the Soul*[4].

The Medical Resonance Music Therapy® CDs composed by Peter Hubner (see Chapter 5 for more information) have in them the elements necessary to stimulate the mind, body, emotions, *and* spirit. The preparations are created by using all of the elements of music to their greatest effect, along with the highest of intent from the composer.

Another interesting set of CDs for the soul come from Uri Harel who has produced what he calls "Music from God". Each Hebrew letter in selections from eight Psalms as well as the "Song of Moses" from the Book of Exodus was assigned a tonal value according to a scheme grounded in Gematria (the science of the numerical values of the Hebrew letters) and Hebrew tradition. Then the text was 'translated' from a series of letters to a series of musical notes. Very talented, well-known musicians, with careful attention to sequence, phrasing, word breaks and vowel-sounds, scored the melody found in the text, and then produced a full-range musical piece from each one of the chapters translated. In addition, there was a discovery of unexpected symbols imbedded in the sound tracks of certain words. For example: when played on a computer, the sound track of the word "Hallelujah" produced on the screen a series of "Star of David" symbols. This unusual phenomenon could be seen as another confirmation that this specific combination must have a special meaning.

There are many anecdotal testimonies of healing, effortless relaxation, and easier concentration. Reactions range from babies sleeping more soundly, to a calming effect on children's behavior, to adults and older people who report a profound spiritual experience. For more information: www.MusicfromGod.com.

Soulfilled Performances

As a musician I have felt the power of soul music both when listening and when performing. In all cases, for me, I become overpowered with the sounds, cannot talk, usually experience tears flowing if not outright sobbing, feel energy rushing or tingles, and often visualize other places and events. This has happened as I played flute in an orchestra and then as I sang in large choruses or a small acapella group. Sometimes I could control it, most times not. So much for being a professional musician! I still cannot sing *Silent Night* without my throat closing and tears flowing. There are other times when playing my flute or piano that I feel I am at one with the music, as if it is playing through me. And sometimes I am in my head just focusing on the notes. The first would be an example of a soulfilled performance, the second, a performance that may be technically perfect but lacking 'something'. The first time I became aware of the phenomena of the performer influencing the music was hearing the same Chopin waltz played by Artur Rubenstein and Vladimer Horowitz. The notes were the same notes, but I fell in love with Rubenstein's performance. A few years later I was attending a workshop given by the pianist and Sufi Alludin Mathieu. He gave the exact example I had noticed and explained the difference as: some performers are wa-wa performers, i.e. they are technically great. But other performers are both technically proficient and they play from their soul; they are WA-WA performers. This is not quite a scientific explanation, but the point was made. A performer reads the composer's score, which shows the essential contours of the music, and tries to reproduce them with the utmost conviction and to play as technically correct as possible. The WA-WA performer, or musical adept, then applies her imagination and allows her to connect with the collective unconscious, the Divine, the Flow. Since then I have talked to many other musicians who are able to distinguish this same feeling, and we agree on the same performers we want to listen to. Kurt Leland calls this phenomenon 'radiance'.

So, not only are there compositions that have inherent in them the energies of our collective unconscious or the Divine as imbrued by a visionary composer, but the performer(s) adds to these energies with her own ability to be in that flow. Another example was my hearing the Barber *Adagio for Strings* played by both the Israel Symphony conducted by Zuben Mehta and then the Tokyo Symphony. This is one of my all time favorite soul music pieces and I was dumbfounded when I had absolutely no reaction to it when I heard the Tokyo Symphony play it in a concert. I then sought out the Israel Symphony recordings with Mehta and felt the old familiar sparkles.

There are many soul performers, famous and not so famous, whose recordings you might enjoy. Some that I recommend are: recent San Francisco Symphony and the San Francisco Symphony Chorus recordings are excellent; the cellist Yo Yo Ma; Claudio Abbado and the Vienna Philharmonic recordings; Artur Rubenstein playing Chopin waltzes, the violinists Yehudi Menuhin and Joshua Bell.

Using Soul Music for Healing

I wholeheartedly agree with Peter Hubner's statement: *No healing can take place without addressing the soul.* If you wish to heal, stay healthy, and connect with the Divine, you must include in your daily life, music that touches your Soul. Using music is one of the fastest and most pleasant ways to make this connection. My definition of 'healing music' would include tonal music that helps to harmonize and improve each aspect of self. It is music whose composition was inspired and motivated by ideals. It is music that assists in moving the listener in an upward direction, i.e. expands one's consciousness and heart. Most of the classical music listed in the appendix is 'soul' music, though there are certain emphasized components in each composition itself that place it in a particular category (such as Raising Energy, Cognitive, or Health related).

When I was working in a general hospital several years ago, I remember a 45-year old female patient in ICU who was very slowly dying and no one could figure out why. She was attached to every life support modern medicine had and nothing was changing. I suggested to her nurse that she play a tape I had compiled for the hospital of 'soul' music, thinking that if she indeed was in the process of transitioning to the next life, hearing beautiful music might assist her. I wasn't able to reconnect with the nurse for a few days, but when I did I was informed that the patient had been moved to a regular room in the hospital and was doing quite well. Apparently she had begun to stabilize and then improve some hours after the nurse had started the soul music tape. The patient never talked about her experience.

The use of soul music can have dramatic results, many times leaving the person unable to find words to describe the experience. I would give the soul music tape to anyone who was psychologically depressed, for whatever reason. It always elicits tears and moves the person to another level. An example was the middle age man in a CCU unit who was depressed and not responding to any human intervention. His nurse gave him the soul music tape and within 10 minutes he was sobbing and tore off the headphones stating he didn't want any more of that music. His nurse quietly asked him if he wanted to talk about it. This led to an hour conversation and the patient's disclosure of his life as an alcoholic and an incident where he nearly beat his son to death. This happened 20 years previously after which he walked out of his house and had never seen his family again. His physical condition stabilized after this event and he sought counseling to assist him on his journey. The keys to the success of this intervention were in first using the 'soul' music to stimulate an opening, and then the nurse proactively encouraging him to talk while she listened to his story.

I saw a sign once: **Feel good music**   I encourage you to.

[1] Zatorre, Robert. "Music and Emotions". 12/02, Institute for Music and Neurologic Function Conference: "Dialogues Across Disciplines: Cognitive Neuroscience and Music Processing in Human Function.

[2] Jung, Carl. *The Spirit in Man, Art and Literature.* Princeton, N.J.: Princeton University Press. 1966.

[3] Tame, David. *The Secret Power of Music.* N.Y.: Destiny Books. 1984.

[4] Leland, Kurt. *Music and the Soul.* Charlottesville VA: Hampton Roads Publishing Co. 2005

CHAPTER 7

SOUND AS THERAPY

Imagine yourselves out there in the universe. From all the heavenly bodies it is singing, speaking as it sings, singing as it speaks, and all your perception is a listening to this speech which is song, and the singing speech of the Cosmos...And whenever a planet in its course passes a constellation of the fixed stars, there bursts forth, not one single note, but a whole world of music.
Thus we have in the heavens of the fixed stars a wondrous Cosmic instrument of MUSIC.   Rudolf Steiner

The Sound of Creation

In the Christian Bible, the book of Genesis tells us that creation began when God spoke the words, "Let there be light," and the Gospel of John also asserts/claims/proclaims that sound is the author of all things: "In the beginning was the Word, and the Word was with God, and the Word was God...All things were made by him." However, hundreds of years before Christianity, the immortal words of the Hindu Vedas said: "In the beginning was Brahman with whom was Vak, or the Word, and the Word is Brahman." In Egypt, the ancients believed that Thoth spoke the world into life by naming an object and bringing it into life. And on the North American continent, the Hopi Indian legend says Spider Woman sang the song of creation over inanimate forms on earth and brought them to life.

The mystical traditions of Egypt, Rome, Greece, Tibet and India tell us that sound is the very fount from which our universe sprang. It is responsible for creation, as well as sustaining and transforming all life and all matter. These traditions knew of the effects of sound, which was a highly refined science. All of them used vocal sounds to activate energy in the body for healing. The Pythagorean School and Philosophy, which lasted over 800 years, taught that music was equal in importance to mathematics and, again, was the foundation of all things.

Likewise, the Jewish mystics, known as Kabbalists, taught that the Divine Word, the speech of God, creates and sustains both the heavens and the earth. They, too, believed that the various objects in our universe are different because a specific and unique combination of letters of sacred speech sustains each one.

The Power of the Voice

In Africa, the Sangomas (Shamans in the Congo) heal the sick, bring on rainstorms, ease the pain of childbirth, and calm the fury of raging animals with the utterance of a single word or phrase. There are also many stories of some of our Native American medicine men, Rolling Thunder for one, who have used words and chants to bring about changes in weather and health and to manifest objects. There are several Sound Healers today who are reviving ancient chants for the purposes of creating health and prosperity. Three of the most well known are: Jonathan Goldman (www.healingsounds.com), Jeffery Thompson, Ph.D. (www.neuroacoustic.com), and Mitchell Gibson, M.D. (www.tybro.com). They use the power of the voice as a potent instrument for the restoration and maintenance of optimal health. Goldman, as well as some other sound healers, is able to direct his voice to different parts of a person's body to bring it back 'in tune'. Also, like Dr. Gibson, he has recorded several ancient chants onto CDs. His *Holy Harmony* CD uses the ancient Hebrew words for God combined with precisely tuned tuning forks for a very beautiful and inspiring album. Dr. Gibson's CDs use ancient Hebrew chants to align a person to such things as prosperity, miracles, and healing. Dr. Thompson records a person's own voice and mixes it with specific tones that increase relaxation. Listening to this combination creates a mix of emotions such as love, caring, and safety and feelings of comfort and relaxation to assist in healing.

In his research with the tonoscope, Swiss scientist Dr Hans Jenny[1] noticed that when the vowels of the ancient languages of Hebrew and Sanskrit were pronounced, sand placed on a metal plate vibrated and took the shape of the written symbols for these vowels, while our modern languages, on the other hand, did not generate the same result. How is this possible? Did the ancient Hebrews and Indians know this? Is there something to the concept of "sacred language," which both of these are sometimes called? What qualities do these "sacred languages," among which Tibetan, Sanskrit, Egyptian and Hebrew possess?

Toning

For centuries the early Christian church prohibited the use of musical instruments in the church. It was the belief that the human voice was the most perfect instrument for creating music. In his book *Healing Sounds*[2], Jonathan Goldman explores many of the vocal traditions on our planet from Tibetan overtone chanting, where the voice is trained to produce more than one note at a time, to current toning and chanting used to rebalance the body. He recounts many research findings that demonstrate the effect of using one's voice or having a sound healer's voice directed at you. These include beneficial changes in respiration, cranial bones, the brain, rate of flow of cerebral spinal fluid, and the pineal gland. This is a further demonstration of how sound can affect our body symphony.

Over the years there has been some refinement of the types of sounds that are effective to use when toning. It appears that lower sounds influence lower parts of the body, as higher sounds influence the upper body. There also appears to be a direct relationship between specific vowels and different parts of the body. For instance, to decrease fatigue and increase energy, sit up straight, take a deep breath, and slowly sing a high note on the vowel 'aye' or 'eeee' and imagine sending it to your brain. Remember to sing with some energy! Do this for no more than 5 minutes. For relaxation: sit up straight, take a deep breath, and slowly sing a low note on the vowel sound "uh" or 'ah' and send it to your lower abdomen. Again, put some energy into your sound.

Sound researcher and musician Fabian Maman[3] has shown in his work how the voice affects cancer cells. First he applied one or two notes played on a variety of instruments to Hela cancer cells. In the last series of experiments he used the human voice singing the C scale. He took photographs of isolated cells with an ordinary camera fixed on the microscope. The most dramatic results occurred when he used the combination of the human voice and the musical scale. The Hela cells exploded more rapidly and predictably.

In the Tibetan chanting tradition, many of the monks create more than one note at a time, called overtone chanting. It appears that both the listener and the producer of this type of singing benefit greatly. Mark Rider[4], Ph.D. found decreases in heart rate, respiration and brain wave activity as well as a charging of the cortex of the brain during overtone chanting. This translates to being able to relax and often go into very deep meditative states. For those of you interested in hearing overtone chanting, David Hykes, founder of the Harmonic Choir, has a very effective and interesting CD, *Solar Winds*. (www.harmonicworld.com)

The Physics of Sound

In the 21st century, we are proving what these ancient groups had known. The field of Quantum Physics is demonstrating that all of creation is composed of vibration which when lowered in frequency to our hearing range, is sound. Everything is waves of energy or vibration, or inaudible sound. As a protective measure, our physical hearing is such that we are unable to hear most things vibrate--can you imagine what it would be like if you could! Instead, we have very sensitive microscopes so our eyes can see everything vibrating. As we peer into the microscope at the first layer we can see the molecules moving, although some, like molecules in wood or stone, do not move much. But as we look further, we see the protons, neutrons, and electrons vibrating, and inside the proton we see quarks dancing.

We are a walking symphony of sound: heartbeat, rushing blood, digestion, and vibrating cells all playing together to form you. Every thing has a resonant frequency or number of cycles per second that it vibrates. For instance, the resonant frequency of water might be 100 cycles per second. If the molecules dance faster or slower, the water changes its tune and becomes something different, for example, steam or ice. The human heart has a certain resonant frequency, as does each muscle and vertebra, hormone, and cell salt. When any of these vibrate too fast or too slow, we become out of tune and might feel sick or uncomfortable.

The field of Cymatics (www.cymaticsource.com), pioneered by Swiss scientist Dr. Hans Jenny in the 1950's, is the science of how sound waves translate into physical patterns. He conducted experiments that directed simple pure tones into powders, pastes, and liquids. Abrasive sounds created abstract, fragmented, scattered and lopsided images. Harmonic sounds transformed the materials into patterns that are found throughout nature: crystals, chromosomes, cells, molecules, bone, and tissue. However, as the frequency was raised in pitch, the images cracked and fell apart in chaos. As the frequency continued to be raised the images organized again into beautiful patterns. His research demonstrated that each cell generates its own frequency and the nature of the frequency determines what the resulting structure will be, i.e. heart, ruby, or pine needle. Growth is the result of the vibrations. Here was the scientific demonstration of the ancients' belief that all is composed of sound and sound can influence matter. What Hans Jenny pointed out in his book *Cymatics-- The Structure and Dynamics of Waves and Vibrations* (1974) is the resemblance between the shapes and patterns we see around us in physical reality and the shapes and patterns he generated in his investigations.

Jenny was convinced that biological evolution was a result of vibrations, and that their nature determined the ultimate outcome. He speculated that every cell had its own frequency and that a number of cells with the same frequency created a new frequency that was in harmony with the original, which in its turn possibly formed an organ that also created a new frequency in harmony with the two preceding ones. Jenny was saying that the key to understanding how we can heal the body with the help of tones lies in our understanding of how different frequencies influence genes, cells and various structures in the body. This is the basis of quantum physics.

Influencing the basic frequency of an object

One of the ways the basic frequency of an object can be altered is through <u>entrainment.</u> In this process, the powerful rhythmic vibrations of one object will cause the less powerful vibrations of another object of similar frequency to lock in step and oscillate with the more powerful object. If several clocks are started at approximately the same time, all will entrain their motions to the loudest clock, and will soon be tick-tocking together. The use of entrainment is not a new technique. In his book *The Healing Gods of Ancient Civilizations* (1962), physician Walter Jayne states that the ancient Egyptian and Greek civilizations were using these principles and techniques for healing in their temples.

Another way of changing a frequency is to match the resonant frequency of an object and <u>implode</u> it, break it up. An opera singer who sings a note that has the same frequency as a crystal wine glass creates a resonance that may shatter the glass, just as the construction industry uses sound to break up concrete. Another example can be found in modern medicine where ultrasound is used to break up kidney stones.

A third method of influencing the basic frequency of an object is through <u>dissonance.</u> It appears that cancer cells, at least, can be destabilized and led to explosion by the introduction of a sequence of notes. The accumulation of the sounds creates an intolerable dissonance within the cell.[5]

Advantages of Using Sound

The therapeutic application of frequencies appears to have several advantages over music and traditional medicine.

First, frequencies may be applied to specific areas of the body that need attention thereby eliminating the possibility of effecting surrounding or related body parts and processes.

Second, the frequencies bypass all the personal and cultural musical biases of the patient.

Third, the application of frequencies is controllable and the outcome measurable as a direct correlation. When a frequency is applied, there are definite physiological reactions such as change in heart rate, blood pressure, oxygenation, and change in the targeted body part. When applying frequencies to a person attached to a pulse oxymeter, you can watch the changes in blood pressure and oxygen saturation occurring as a direct correlation to the sound applied. Dr. Jeffery Thompson, sound researcher and chiropractor, does a chemical blood screen before and after his sound sessions. When using sound to realign the vertebrae, it corrected chemical imbalances noted prior to the back being put into place. He also noted, that when he played a frequency that an organ fully resonated at, a chemical blood screen that determined one's nutritional needs, also corrected itself. (more information is at www.neuroacoustic.org.

And fourth, treatment appears to be painless, with no negative side effects *when* applied in a prescribed manner.

SOUND THERAPIES - these are just a few of the many techniques that are being employed today. The field of sound therapy is developing so quickly that is difficult to keep up with the amazing amount of creativity and research.

Tuning Forks

Tuning forks are an extremely valuable tool for any practitioner. Sets of tuning forks are tuned for use in different ways. The ratios or intervals are important to consider when using them. For example, the notes of C and G have been shown to have the greatest therapeutic applications. Set the two forks to vibrating and hold one next to each ear about 3 inches away. After about three seconds move the tuning forks to the opposite ears. It can bring about synchronization of the hemispheres and feelings of relaxation and well-being. When feeling stressed, just give yourself a one-minute tune up with the forks. (See Appendix C for references).

Another type of tuning fork is called the resonator. The fork has a resonating disk on the end of each tine that assists in prolonging and amplifying the sound. The C 64Hz resonator is particularly effective when applied to sore points on the body. When the reflexologist in our clinic used it on the base of her thumbs, pain disappeared after 20 minutes and did not return until she overused them again.

One of the first persons to use tuning forks in his healing practice is John Beaulieu, N.D., Ph.D. He was using tuning forks 25 years ago in Bellevue Hospital in New York City. He found that the tuning forks were calming and relaxing to his patients. Since then, he has formulated a system of BioSonic Repatterning uses tuning forks of different intervals struck and moved around the head. (for more information: www.biosonics.com)

Acutonics, a system formulated by Dona Carey and Marjorie de Muynck, uses tuning forks of specific frequencies and musical intervals that are tuned to the Orbital Properties of the Earth, Moon, Sun and other Planets. Pairs of these tuning forks are prescribed and placed on specific acupuncture points. The stem resonates in the physical layer of the body on the acupuncture point when spreads through the meridian. The vibration of sound travels faster than the vibration of an acupuncture needle. The tines of the fork are resonating in the etheric layer where dis-ease begins. (See more at www.acutonics.com).

Fabian Maman, the French musician and sound researcher, is also an acupuncturist, but uses tuning forks. He has discovered the exact frequency for each acupuncture Shu point, Mu point on the back, and ear and foot reflexology points. His tuning forks match the frequencies he uses on the acupuncture points. (More information at www.tama-do.com)

SomaEnergetics

The standard Western musical scale today is very different from the original scale used in music. It is a twelve-tone equal temperment that allows us to change from one key to another without needing to retune our instruments. Before this equal tuning, orchestras could only play compositions in the same key. To come to the equal tuning, each pitch was changed from the original scale so that all notes are a little out of tune. In *Healing Codes for the Biological Apocalypse*[6], the frequency numbers for the original Solfeggio scale was found to be encoded in the Bible in Numbers 7:12-83.

David Hulse developed a healing technique, SomaEnergetics, that uses the ancient Solfeggio scale to balance and restore energy. He uses tuning forks tuned to produce the original frequency and chanting which opens people to divine inspiration, revelation, wisdom an knowledge. When comparing the Solfeggio scale frequencies to the current scale we see many interesting changes, for example, the third note originally was 528 Hz and today it is 512Hz. We know that 528Hz is a frequency that assists in repairing our DNA!

David believes that "through the Solfeggio tones, people can open channels of energy within and allow their life force energy to flow freely. This is what the Solfeggio Frequencies were originally supposed to accomplish." David uses the six original tones found in Numbers. From his research he determined that these frequencies were used for:

Scale syllable	Frequency in Hertz	Purpose of the Frequency
UT	396	Turning grief to joy: Liberating guilt and fear
RE	417	Helping a person to connect to their source to bring forth miracles; undoing situations and facilitating changes.
MI	528	DNA repair and transformation
FA	639	Connecting with spiritual family relationships
SOL	741	Solving situations and increasing Intuition
LA	852	Returning to spiritual order

Other researchers believe that the above scale is incomplete and have added three more frequencies: 174, 285, and 961. They believe these additional frequencies complete evolutionary pathways in our consciousness.

The beautiful tones can be heard on "Paint Your Soul" CD at www.jillswingsoflight.com and on Jonathan Goldman's "Holy Harmony" at www.healingsounds.com. A CD of the pure tones is found at www.healthyworlddistributing.com.

Cyma Therapy

The therapeutic application of cymatics (the science of how sound waves translate into physical patterns) is currently being researched in England and the U.S. The basic principle operative in cymatics therapy is entrainment. The healthy frequency of the body part to be treated, having been predetermined, is incorporated into a harmonic of five frequencies, which is applied through the skin by an "applicator" to specific acupuncture points on the body. The sounds produced are attuned to the body's natural frequencies. Although the approach is only 30 or so years old, successes have been demonstrated in cases of rheumatism, arthritis, fracture, muscle strain, and many other afflictions. The leading pioneer in this area is Dr. Peter Guy Manners. (www.cymatherapy.com)

Vibro Tactile Stimulation

Today there are several sound tables/chairs available. Somatron, Betar, So Sound, Klini Soundwave, Vibroacoustics, and Dr. Jeffery Thompson's are a few of the current names of tables that have speakers embedded in them. Lying on the bed, one can feel the vibrations of music, a condition known as sensory resonance when all the senses receive simultaneous stimulation. This assists in freeing up mental energy that would normally be used to screen out countless irritating background sensations and assists in decreasing physical symptoms. Researchers point out that musical frequencies, when experienced through the table or chair, are perceived not only by our ears and skin, but also by our spinal cored and brain, and therefore potentially by all parts of our bodies. Vibro-tactile tables and chairs are being used in hospitals, universities, schools, mind/brain centers, and private and governmental facilities across the world. (See list of research citations at end of this chapter). Clinical reports demonstrate some interesting results including: the complete elimination of migraine, sinus and tension headaches; decrease in pain during invasive cancer procedures; decrease in anxiety, muscle tension, and spasticity; assistance in entering into deep relaxation faster; and a consistent ability to summon and soothe individual personalities of those suffering from multiple personality disorders.

The nature of the sonic treatment on the bed is essentially dependent on what music comes through the speakers. Children's Cancer Center in Tampa FL finds soothing music that has a mother's heartbeat embedded in it to be effective both before and after painful invasive procedures. In a study[7] designed to reduce stress headaches, Native American flute music ("Canyon Trilogy" by Carlos Nakai) was found to be successful. Other music found to be influential includes: Baroque music with autism, any of the Hemi-Sync music tapes (www.InnerHarmonyHealthCenter.com), and in general, music that is non-percussive, slow, melodious, and has a strong bass line. Many harpists are now connecting their instruments to the tables and intuitively playing music that assists their clients. David Ison (www.Therasound.com) has been composing specific music for the Somatron and Vibroaccoustic tables that has been consistently successful.

The Betar, So Sound chair and mats, the Vibroacoustics table and mat, the Klini SoundWave chair, and Dr. Jeffery Thompson's sound table are equipped with specially designed low frequency, solid steel transducers, comparable to electronic tuning forks, attached to a hardwood or carbon underside of the table or chair. When lying on this padded tuning board, a person feels and becomes part of the sound vibration through direct bone conduction. As many say, "It is an awesome experience." To magnify and spread the sound more evenly throughout the entire body mass, geometrically engineered resonance chambers are used. The transducers and resonance chambers are mathematically arranged for the highest resonance of the body.

The Thompson™ Audio Program Recordings and the So Sound CDs (from www.SoSoundSolutions.com) have been technologically engineered with precision low frequency vibrations to most effectively resonate the body and entrain the brain into different states of consciousness for stress reduction, holistic healing, deep relaxation, emotional release, enhanced therapeutic interaction, openness, and meditation. These specific low frequency sound waves give the optimal effect of vibration through the body and hence, set the stage for the true holistic healing.

Vibroacoustic Therapy

In 1959 Dr. Teirich built a couch containing loudspeakers that had a response range from 20hz-60hz for generating vibration into the back. Clients reported warmth in the solar plexus, warmth throughout the body, floating sensations caused by the bass tones, relaxation in the region of the stomach, dreamlike states, and images. In the 1980's, Norwegian educator and therapist Olav Skille, constructed a unit that he initially described as a "music bath" that bathed his subjects in sound and music. He found some success in helping children who were severely physically and mentally impaired to achieve relaxation. This process consisted of playing music and sine wave tones through speakers into a mattress filled with semi-soft pellets. Patients lying on the mattress feel the vibrations throughout their bodies. He found that the most significant frequencies range between 40-80HZ. For instance, 40 hz was predominantly felt in the thighs and legs, 50 Hz was more significantly felt in the coccyx, sacrum, and lower lumbar region, and 60 Hz was typically felt in the thoracic area and to some extent in the lumbar region. Dr. Skille noticed several effects with his patients: weakened spasticity, a rise in activity level, a lessening or disappearance of stress-related shoulder pains; reduction in lumbago-type back pains and other muscular tension; and reduction in back-area menstrual pain [8]. Since then, a variety of clinical conditions have been treated with Vibroacoustic Therapy in Norway, England, Finland, Estonia, and the U.S. The process of giving Vibroacoustic Therapy involves the use of recorded music and specific low frequency tones, played through an amplifier and delivered to the body via sound table, chair or mat. Some of these conditions include: autism, pulmonary disorders, asthma, spastic conditions, anxiety, and neurosis. Chairs and mats need to be carefully constructed for this modality to be effective. The Vibroacoustic website offers an approved mat (http://vibroacoustic.org). See Appendix F for specific research references.

Tomatis Method

Auditory assessment for the purposes of sound therapy was founded by Alfred A. Tomatis, a French physician and ear/nose/throat specialist. Sound therapy is based upon the idea that the body requires the presence of a full range of harmonious frequencies working cooperatively. A dramatic story involving Dr. Tomatis demonstrates this principle.

83

"Once Dr. Tomatis was called to an abbey where the monks had lost their spirit, some having given up monastic life altogether. Those who stayed were feeling more and more tired; many suffered from all sorts of physical and psychological problems and never left their room...

The monks tried to solve their problem themselves. The first thing they had done was eliminate the night vigil and sleep all night long, believing that a good night's sleep is the best remedy for tiredness. As a result of oversleeping, they became more tired. They then decided to consult various physicians. Each one came, made a diagnosis and wrote out prescriptions. One physician decided that their vegetarian diet was a fault and suggested that they eat meat. The monks were still tired, so vitamins were added to their diet. Then came all sorts of medications. However, the religious men still felt ill and continued to leave the monastery.

When his turn came, Tomatis attacked the problem from the point of view of the ear. He found out that with the changes that occurred after the Second Vatican council of 1960, the monks had decided to stop singing Gregorian Chant...

To re-energize the monks, Tomatis recommended the reintroduction of Gregorian chant. It was difficult for many of the monks to follow this suggestion. After all, singing is the last think you feel like doing when you are depressed. To "awaken" the ear again, a sound stimulation program with the help of the Electronic Ear was suggested for most of the monks. The great majority regained their physical and spiritual health after following the program."[9]

From this story we can see that singing gives us energy. The voice is a source of sound, the ear is the receiver of sound and together they form a dynamic system. Tomatis believes that during gestation the brain is developed from the pattern of the first organ to form: the ear. Early in his work, Tomatis discovered learning is dependent on our hearing. He found that the right ear is the dominant listening ear since it has more connections with the left side of the brain that understands language, and that the neural link between the left brain and the larynx is shorter. He discovered that when the right ear is not in a position of control there is no leading ear at all. Hesitant and monotonous speech may occur, possibly stammering or even stuttering. In most children with language and learning problems, the right ear did not develop as the leading ear. His method therefore addresses specific problems of listening, not hearing.

After assessing the listening strengths and weaknesses, the ear is introduced to filtered sound stimulations through special equipment. The chief objective of the passive phase is to recreate the prenatal environment by means of sounds rich in high frequencies. The sounds are usually a combination of mother's recorded voice and music by Mozart. The ear is forced to expand its range of perception and increase its selective powers. The program then progresses to an active phase of voice exercises including first singing and chanting, then word and sentence repetition, and finally a read aloud phase. [10]

Many language, speech, and learning disabilities, thought to be irreversible, including ADD and ADHD, are currently being altered. Even some behavior problems and motor skills can be improved with increased listening abilities. Some of the specific changes that have occurred are:

    accelerated learning

    increase in information integration

    improved vocal range and hearing

    reversal of several behavioral problems such as attention, concentration, memory, aggression, hyperactivity and regressive tendencies

    problems with lateral dominance and handedness

    and reversal of learning disabilities and problems with reading, writing, spelling and calculation.

BioAcoustics

BioAcoustics is an exciting new field within Subtle Energy Medicine. It is built on a foundation of three decades of research at Sound Health Alternatives, Inc. BioAcoustics can most aptly be described as a cross between music therapy and biofeedback. It is based on the premise that all living systems emit frequencies termed "Signature Sounds". These Signature Sounds are an indication of each person's physical and emotional status, as well as a reflection of any stress residing in a body's frequencies. In this therapy, analysis of the voice is used to identify and interpret the constant, complicated frequency interactions within the body. The technique demonstrates that the frequencies contained in the vocal patterns provide a holographic representation of the human body. Sharry Edwards is the founder and primary researcher in this area. Her preliminary studies indicate that when a person's missing sounds are returned to his/her environment, the body begins to rebuild itself--even from the so-called "incurable" diseases. The technique consists of a voice spectral analysis and the deliverance of specific frequencies in the brain wave range through headphones and tone box, or subwoofer, or vibro-tactile chair/table. Although it is still in its infancy, frequency formulas based on a person's Signature Sounds have assisted in attaining positive results in cases of lung ailments, broken bones, eye problems, epileptic seizures, heart conditions, high blood pressure, metal toxicity, hyperostosis, diabetes, Down syndrome, genetic syndromes, MS, chronic and traumatic pain, attention/learning disorders, and many more. The Inner Harmony website carries many frequency CD programs that focus on specific diseases and symptoms that can be listened to through headphones, i.e. *Digest Aid, Spinal Ease, Knee Aid, Stress Buster,* and others. (www.InnerHarmonyHealthCenter.com)

Hemi-Sync

In the 1930's, German experimenter H.S. Dove discovered the phenomenon of binaural beats. These are beats that are generated in the human brain as a result of hearing different externally generated frequencies in each ear. For instance, if a tone of 200 beats per minute was played in the right ear and a tone of 210 beats in the left, the brain would "hear" the difference in the beats and generate its own frequency of 10 beats per minute. No one ever "hears" the binaural beats per minute.[11] The late Robert Monroe, formerly a composer in the communications industry, used this theory to develop an auditory guidance system to heighten selected awareness and performance while establishing a relaxed state. Using entrainment principles, specific frequencies sent to each ear assist in entraining the separate areas of the hemispheres to equal electromagnetic environments to enhance the free-flowing exchange of information between hemispheres. The resulting synchronicity of the hemispheres greatly increases learning, healing, meditative abilities, i.e., when the brain waves are in a particular frequency and left and right hemispheres are synchronized, optimal functioning occurs.

Research at the Monroe Institute in Faber, Virginia indicates that an optimal brain wave state might be in the "theta state", when an individual is very relaxed and highly receptive and uncritical. States of consciousness are differentiated by brain wave pattern:

Beta(14-100 Hz)	Normal waking consciousness; alert, analytic Higher levels associated with anxiety, dis-ease
Alpha(8-14 Hz)	Alert but unfocused, relaxed, light trance, pre-sleep, Meditation, increased serotonin production
Theta (4-8 Hz)	REM sleep, trance, deep meditation, uncritical, Optimal learning state, creative, integrative
Delta(.1-4 Hz)	Deep dreamless sleep, access to unconscious, loss of body awareness

The greatest practical problem with the efficacy of the theta state is an individual's tendency to slide down into delta (sleep). To assist in achieving this state, a special mix of frequencies is used. These are embedded in ocean surf sounds, "pink noise", or non-rhythmical music recorded onto tapes/CDs. The actual tones are inaudible, as hearing them would be irritating. There are dozens of CDs with specific purposes: deep relaxation; pain reduction or decreasing other physical symptoms; improving performances such as sports, concentration and memory. The results from regular usage of the programs can be dramatic, as the brain is trained to operate at an optimal level. With respect to healing, it appears we can consciously learn to control various aspects of our physiology when we are in the theta state.

Sound Caution

With the availability and ability to purchase sound producing equipment there needs to be an emphasis on caution. Just as there are beneficial ways to use sound for healing, the opportunity is also present to use sound to harm. One practitioner I knew was convinced that listening to two different pieces of music simultaneously through headphones and in a sound chair was highly effective at disorganizing the body and therefore eliciting a shift toward wellness. My first experience caused a shift all right – into nausea and dizziness. This goes against the Hippocratic Oath regarding 'first, do no harm'.

The most memorable story I read of sound doing harm was recounted in Randall McClellan's book *The Healing Forces of Music.* [12] French engineer, Professor Gavraud, built a sis-foot long version of the French police pea whistle powered with compressed air. When a short blast was given, many of Gavraud's assistants died of ruptured livers. When Gavraud died (of natural causes) all blueprints for the instruments were banned, his laboratory was disbanded, and all photographs were confiscated by the French government. There are many other examples of the destructive potential of vibration in Lyall Watson's book *Supernature*. [13] Most recently there have been several stories[14] on the harm done to marine mammals during underwater naval sonar and seismic tests. The AP wire service carried a story on Israel's newest weapon against Jewish settlers who resist Gaza Strip evacuation.[15] "The Scream", a device that emits penetrating bursts of sound, leaves its targets reeling with dizziness and nausea. The special frequency targets the inner ear. A spokesperson from the Global Security think tank said he believes it is possible that China, Russia, and the U.S. are developing acoustic weapons.

[1] Jenny, Hans. *Cymatics Vol. I&II*. Basilus, 1974.
[2] Goldman, Jonathan. *The Healing Sounds: the Power of Harmonics*. Element, 1996.
[3] Maman, Fabien. *The Role of Music in the 21st Century*. Tama-Do Press, 1997..
[4] Rider, Mark. *The Rhythmic Language of Health and Disease*. St. Louis, MO: MMB Music, Inc.1997.
[5] Mamon, Ibid.
[6] Horowitz and Puleo. *Healing Codes for a Biological Apololypse*. Tetra Hedron Publishing, Idaho. 2001.
[7] Wigram, T. and Dileo, C. (Eds). *Music Vibration*. Cherry Hill, NJ: Jeffrey Books, 1997.
[8] Skille, Olav. "The Music Bath." in *Angst, Schmerz, Musik in der Anasthesie*. 1983.
[9] Madaule, Paul. *When Listening Comes Alive*. Moulin Publishing. Norval, Ont. 1993
[10] Madaule, Paul. Ibid.
[11] Atwater, F. Holmes. "The Monroe Institute's Hemi-Sync Process". Working paper available from The Monroe Institute, Box 175, Faber, VA 22938. 1988.
[12] McClellan, Randall. *The Healing Forces of Music* Rockport MA, Element, Inc. 1991.
[13] Watson, Lyall. *Supernature*. Garden City, N.Y., Anchor Press, 1973.
[14] www.masternewmedia.org/news/2005/01/25/underwater_seismic_testing_linked_t o.htm
[15] Teibel, Amy. "Israel May Use Sound Weapon on Settlers". AP News, June 10, 2005

CHAPTER 8

APPLICATIONS OF MUSIC
FOR PAIN REDUCTION AND IN SURGERY

Music, sweet Music, come take me
Flying so high on your love
Winged bright angel of beauty
One guide, one light, from above....
Usman Friedman

The current field of Music Therapy is a broad one, encompassing psychotherapeutic, educational, instructional, behavioral, pastoral, supervisory, healing, recreational activity, and interrelated arts applications of music and sound. The use of music and sound in medicine is rapidly growing and being recognized once again as a viable treatment modality. The newest branch of Music Therapy is Medical Music Therapy, most commonly referred to as MusicMedicine. In this application, music is used in medical specialties to:

1) affect health directly,
2) support or enhance medical treatment or procedures,
3) combine in equal importance with a therapist or medical treatment,
4) become part of the therapeutic relationship,
5) and to reduce distress related to specific illnesses.

The International Society for Music in Medicine conferences demonstrate the wide variety of applications and research in this field from analgesia to urology as does the recent compilation of research in music therapy by both the American Music Therapy Association and CAIRSS. The latter is a bibliographic database of music research literature containing over 11,000 citations from articles published in more than 2,000 different journals in 25 languages in 54 countries. The database is maintained by the Institute for Music Research at the

University of Texas at San Antonio. (Additional research web sites are listed in Appendix C.)

The tremendous value of music in medicine is its ability to simultaneously influence mind, body, spirit, and emotions. Used regularly, like any prescribed medication, music is an effective outlet for feelings of stress; an assistant in clarifying issues, decreasing symptoms and an increasing the body's own healing mechanisms. Some of the biomedical applications of music and sound are:

INCREASE	DECREASE
Coordination	Pain
Muscle Recruitment	Headaches
Mood	Depression and Anxiety
Immune System	Nausea
Blood Pressure	Blood Pressure
Pulse Rate	Pulse Rate
Exhalation Ability	Intercranial Pressure
Muscle Tension	Muscle Tension
Respiration Rate	Respiration rate
Walking speed	Crying
EMG Levels	Use of analgesics
Effects of Anesthesia	Effects of Anesthesia
Grasp Strength	Use of Sedatives
Gait	Hospital Stay

To apply music to physiologic healing, one must follow several decision-making steps.

1) The purpose of the application of music or sound: what does one want the music/sound to do for the patient?

2) Both the patient's mental and physical state must be ascertained, as well as cultural background and possibly age.

3) The choice of the most appropriate music must ALSO take into consideration the specific characteristics of music: tempo, rhythm, instrumentation, volume, etc., as discussed in Chapter 5. Music as therapy in medicine then becomes as prescriptive as pharmaceuticals. A Music Therapy Flow Chart is included in Appendix D to assist in the selection process.

SYMPTOM REDUCTION

Symptom reduction addresses some of the same psycho/physiological symptoms so readily treated with medications: hypertension, anxiety, depression, insomnia, wakefulness, restlessness, bladder function, and pain. In my own experience, all of these symptoms are treatable with music and/or sound. All have been explored in previous chapters (with the exception of bladder function). CDs that I have found particularly useful are listed in Appendix A.

The Music Therapy Regimen

For successfully decreasing symptoms with a hospitalized patient, a music therapy program must be established with the cooperation of the nursing staff. CDs must be listened to on a regular basis to establish new patterns in the body. In order for the music programs to work, they need to be presented to the patients as being just as important as their medications.

Therefore, the listening times must, to some extent, be regimented. For instance, an anxiety music program should include listening to CDs at least three times a day, whether or not the patient is feeling increased anxiety. This helps to re-pattern the body so that future events will not stimulate an anxiety response, or at least a diminished one. Insomnia CDs MUST be listened to every night; pain-control CDs need to be used both when the patient is in a significant amount of pain and when in lesser pain; etc. When programs are faithfully followed, not only are patients able to learn some control over their own functioning, but the need for medications are decreased, other therapies are performed more easily and successfully, and the patient's own sense of hopefulness and control increases.

Pain Control

The word pain comes from the Greek word *poine* which means penalty. It is our physical and emotional bodys' way of telling us to stop doing what ever it is that is causing us discomfort. In MindBody medicine there is most likely a mind connection to all pain; the behavioral medicine psychologist is adept at uncovering the antecedents of a variety of types of pain. And, the opposite is also true, the mind can alleviate pain. One of my most dramatic stories is when I was asked to see a female patient who had a significantly high level of pain in her leg due to gangrene. The attending hospital staff had tried

91

massage, distraction, and high levels of pain killers. I began by asking her to close her eyes and just focus on my voice. I gave her relaxation suggestions and had her visualize her pain as a symbol. Then I guided her to push the pain out of her body through her feet. Her eyes popped wide open and she sat up like a shot. She had actually pushed the pain out and was pain free.

Acute pain is derived from the Italian for *needle*; acute pain means sharp penalty. And the word chronic is from the Greek word *chronos*, meaning time; chronic pain = a long time penalty.

Pain is experienced by the brain and modulated by the brain, and there is always a physical and emotional component to pain. Emotional pain stems from such thoughts as: "I have no control", "I'll never get better", "I'll never work again", or "It's all _____ fault". The emotions involved with these thoughts then increase pain in the physical body.

Physical pain involves increased muscle tension, heart rate, blood pressure, sweating, respiration, release of adrenalin and other hormones, peripheral vasoconstriction, acids in the GI tract and decreased sexual functioning.

There are both external and internal ways of modulating pain. Some of the external modalities include: rubbing, massage, acupuncture, myafascial release, trigger point therapy, heat or cold, ultra-sound, TENS unit or movement therapy. Some of the internal modulators are: analgesics, nerve blocks, meditation, relaxation, hypnosis, imagery, and music/sound.

Pain Control Theories There are currently three theories as to music's effectiveness in relieving suffering.

Gate Control Theory This theory proposes that pain can be influenced by cognitive activities such as anxiety, attention, and suggestion, acting at the earliest levels of sensory transmission. Distraction elicits responses that are incompatible with pain responses, and it is for that reason an effective maneuver for reducing anxiety and, thereby, pain. In other words, one cannot think about two things at once; one focuses either on the pain, or on something else. Music can be an effective method of pain relief through its ability to distract.

In this respect it is important to use music that the patient will listen to. Patients in truly terrible pain are often unable to respond to very soft music. It appears that in these cases of extreme pain, the music must match the level of tension and anxiety in order for it to be an effective relaxant and distracter. In working with leukemia children undergoing a short but extremely painful procedure, researchers found "the children, with few exceptions, clamored for Michael Jackson, and, headphones in place, sailed through the ordeal". I found similar results with chronic pain patients. If the pain level was low, pleasant music and guided relaxation tapes worked well to decrease the pain, but when the pain was rated by them to be above 6.5 on a scale of 1-10, then something else was needed to decrease the pain.

Pleasure Theory - The second theory holds that pain reduction occurs when the patient is distracted enough to listen to certain music perceived as uplifting or relaxing. This music and resulting perception stimulate the brain to release endorphins, natural opiates secreted by the hypothalamus, which relieve pain by acting upon certain receptors in the brain and body. In other words, if the patient in a lower level of pain can be distracted by music she perceives as relaxing and pleasant, then the body will release its own pain medication, and both mind and body will find peace.

Vibrational Theory - A newer theory of pain reduction emerges from Quantum physics. When a part of the body is 'out of tune' and relaying strong pain signals, the vibrational rate of that part is strong, unstable, and chaotic. Gentle slow vibrations of music will not be strong enough to influence it. However, if the vibrations applied are stable and their rate close to that of the pain they will create a resonance that entrains, and the pain will decrease. Music therapist Mark Rider[1] found listening to a formulated music tape that exhibited a definite mood shift from unpleasant to pleasant, and from an unstable 7/8 meter to a comfortable 4/4 meter, significantly reduced pain and muscle tension levels, and stimulated more imagery than the other music (minimalist, jazz, classical, and 'preferred' music) that was tested. It is important to note from this study is that the entrainment tape had the greatest effect but the patients liked it the least. The opposite was also true: the preferred music was liked significantly more than all the other music, but it yielded very little effect in decreasing pain or muscle tension.

Using the theory of entrainment, I compiled a CD[2] for intense pain that contains a short relaxation exercise (distraction principle) followed by highly rhythmical minimalist music to entrain, ending with ocean surf (pleasure/release of endorphins). Patients are instructed on the CD to continue listening to the second track that contains soothing, pleasant classical music. Though the patients stated they did not like the minimalist music, they all have reported significant pain decreases that are lasting, particularly if they listen to both tracks. The total listening time is 30-60 minutes (1-2 tracks), which allows for distraction from the prior state and immersion in the new experience. Rider[3] has also found in his research that the imagery stimulated by the music contributes to the reduction of pain as a further pleasant distraction that deepens the listening experience.

In Summary - for effective use of music to mediate pain, the following must be kept in mind:

1. Have the patient assess the level of pain on a scale of 1-10.

2. If pain is rated 6 or lower, music used should be soothing and pleasant. Patient preference can be used.

3. Music that stimulates pleasant images is a greater pain reducer than new age, rock, or jazz. (See Appendix A for Imagery Producing Music.)

4. Children in high levels of pain do well with their own choice of music.

5. If pain is rated above 6, entrainment CDs produce the greatest effect. When pain is above 6, relaxation music and stimulating music will both increase pain.

6. Listening to a guided exercise pain control CD several times a day assists in keeping pain levels down, AND in learning how to control pain when it arises.

Use of Sound to Reduce Pain

We have all experienced the negative effects of sound as chalk squeals across a blackboard or a jackhammer yammers on our street. Using the laws of physics we can use particular frequencies to decrease pain. The field of Vibroacoustics (discussed in Chapter 7) was the first to formally investigate the effects of specific low frequency sounds to diminish pain. Since then, several sound researchers have corroborated Olav Skille's research and expanded the field to include precise frequencies for different types of pain. There are CDs available at both the Vibroacoustic website (http://vibroacoustic.org) and Inner Harmony (www.InnerHarmonyHealthCenter.com) that target a variety of discomforts. Some pain reducing CDs offered are for: muscles, breathing, spine, Fibromyalgia, digestion, and knees.

Dental Pain

The use of music as an analgesia has been explored to a great extent in dentistry. Studies have shown music and white noise to be equally effective in reducing anxiety, intensity of pain, and the need for anesthesia during dental work. Both forms of audio stimulus, listened to through headphones, distract the patient's attention from the ongoing procedure, demonstrating the Gate Control Theory. Allowing the patient to control the level of sound during procedures is important as a means of tuning out the dental distortion and increasing the relief from pain and anxiety. Most dental audio-analgesia research highlights the importance of patient preference. Dentists wishing to offer their patients tapes need to keep the following in mind:

1. It is best to offer a wide variety of styles of music: classical, semi-classical, popular, rock.

2. Instrumental music is most desirable: piano, cello, harp, and guitar are the most preferred.

3. Avoid lullabies, religious music and folk music.

4. Use music with smooth rhythm and harmony.

5. Use a continuous presentation of short pieces of music.

Childbirth Pain

Several researchers have explored the use of music during childbirth with mixed results. Those studies that attempted to match the expectant mother's preference and Lamaze breathing patterns demonstrated significant findings: music assisted in focusing attention, relaxing, and decreasing pain and anxiety. The patients using this music protocol also reported a decrease in perceived length of labor, and increased frequency of Lamaze home practice. In selecting music one must also consider the increasing tempo, intensity and rhythm of childbirth and vary the music accordingly to mobilize the required energy. Selecting music to be played in the delivery room for the moment of birth assists in the celebration. This music must be carefully selected by the parents to reflect and express their feelings; music that has special meaning or sentimental value to the couple is most useful. I have also read of a Chicago hospital that plays the Brahms *Lullaby* over the speaker system each time a baby is born. Staff report feelings of joy and uplifting each time they hear it. In an atmosphere of suffering, the break allows them to focus on something positive and the music expresses so much more than a verbal announcement.

Surgery

The use of music in the general hospital was first introduced in the operating room. Physicians initially used a piano, then a phonograph, to exclude unintended sounds and reduce preoperative anxiety. Today patients can utilize music and sound through all steps of surgery. One of the pioneer researchers in this area was Helen Bonny, a registered music therapist. Her research and findings conclude that music must be of a sedative nature when used prior to and during surgery, and of a stimulating nature during recovery. The music must include a regular rhythm, predictable dynamics, consonance of harmony, and recognized instrumental vocal timbres. Using her knowledge of music and the collected findings of the effects of music on physiology, she has assembled a series of tapes to be used in ICU, OR, and Recovery rooms. Her findings support prior research in the area of music medicine: a significant reduction in heart rate, blood pressure, anxiety, lowered need for pain medication, lessened depression and irritable behavior. In my own doctoral study with one-day surgery patients, I found the same results.

PreSurgery - Most patients are anxious, apprehensive, and fearful before surgery. If possible, at least two weeks before surgery, the patient should begin listening to a guided relaxation tape to assist in learning the relaxation response. Patients who do so enter the experience more relaxed and less fearful. While a patient is waiting to enter surgery, music acts as a distracter to calm and reduce the fear and anxiety. It has a highly consistent reductive effect on systolic and diastolic blood pressures, pulse rate, and respiration rate. Music should be of a calm nature, in a major key, with no changes of tempo or rhythm, and short pieces grouped together to keep the patient's attention. Light classical and easy listening popular music appear to work best.

IntraOperative - It has been demonstrated by hypno-therapists and several surgeons (Bernie Siegal, MD, in particular) that patients 'hear' on an unconscious level all that occurs in the OR, even when completely anesthetized. During this time, it is important for the patient to wear headphones and listen to slow, pleasant music, both to muffle room sounds and to assist in sedation. It is important for the music to have a strong, even rhythm and a tempo slightly lower than normal heart rate, as the heart will entrain itself to the tempo it hears. At the Carle Heart Center in Urbana Illinois, a harpist is often used during heart procedures. The chief of cardiac electrophysiology,

96

Abraham Kocheril, M.D., finds harp music can assist hearts to beat more normally (given the right choice of music).[4] He believes the resonant vibrations from live harp music may be particularly effective at regulating quivering heart rhythms.

The OR staff, on the other hand, will benefit from more stimulating music to keep them alert. This music needs to be approximately 72 beats per minute, even in tempo, with a strong melodic line. Music from the Baroque period works very well (Bach, Teleman, Handel, Mozart - see selections under Cognitive Music in the Appendix). And surgeons take note, a 1994 study (Blasovich) on the effects of music on cardiovascular reactivity among surgeons concluded that surgeons who routinely listen to music in the OR perform more accurately and more calmly when listening to their preferred music; this certainly demonstrates the need for different music for each task.

Imagery specialist Belleruth Naparstek has produced a surgery CD that has been very effective with patients who have not been able to use a relaxation CD prior to surgery. It combines both music and guided relaxation exercise and suggestions for a successful surgical experience. (www.healthjourneys.com)

PostOperative - Several patients have told me they were happy to have music playing in their ears when they were coming out of anesthesia. They commented on its being more pleasant than other sounds in the Recovery room, and it had a calming influence. I remember one older woman telling me she was so happy to hear the music "because then I knew I wasn't dead"! Music for post-surgery should be somewhat stimulating so as to assist the body in mobilizing energy. Positive results have been reported in substantially reduced pain and anxiety, and a drop in anesthesia requirements by as much as 50%. The studies show no difference in using easy listening music, guided imagery music, or preferred choice music. Also, post-surgical patients who listened to five minutes of their favorite music prior to getting up the first time and during the period while on their feet experienced a reduction in the sensation of lightheadedness.

Effects of Music in Surgery*

Physiological	decreases in BP: diastolic, systolic, & mean
	decreased heart rate
	decreased stress hormone levels
	decreased respiration rates
	decreased muscle tension
	less pain medication needed
	less anesthesia needed
	shorter hospital stay
Behavioral	decreased body movements
	improved facial expressions
	fewer verbal pain reports
	sitting up sooner post surgery
	reduced struggling and delirium
Psychological	satisfaction with music experience

Psychophysiological
    decreased anxiety
    decreased pain
    decreased fatigue
    increased relaxation
    fewer sedatives required

*Effects are increased with the use of Imagery and/or Hemi-Sync

Table 2.

Hemi-Sync - Special mention should be made here of the use of the Emergency Treatment (EMS) series Hemi-Sync tapes, which are specifically composed for surgery. (For a complete discussion of Hemi-Sync see the section in Chapter 7.) Consisting of six guided relaxation and imagery tapes/CDs, the series covers the entire surgical scenario: preoperative relaxation, intra-operative, recovery room, pain control, energy mobilization and a CD of gentle surf sounds. My experience in using both the Hemi-Sync and music CDs has demonstrated the effectiveness of both in different circumstances. For one-day surgical procedures during which the patient will be awake, I have found the combination of a guided relaxation hemi-sync CD (the PreOperative CD) used one to two weeks prior to surgery, and then, appropriate music during the various aspects of surgery (Music Rx IntraOp tape), most effective. For all general anesthesia surgeries, the Emergency Treatment series is highly effective in reducing preoperative anxiety and fear, the amount of anesthesia required, post-operative pain and recovery time, as well as increasing a general sense of well-being and control of one's surgical process. There appears to be a direct correlation between commitment to the Hemi-Sync CD listening and the effect achieved--**the more one listens to the CD, the more beneficial the effects.** I have given the ETS CDs to hundreds of patients now. All who used the PreOperative CD had an effect directly related to the number of times they listened before the surgery. Those who listened every day and even two times a day came into the surgical experience more relaxed, calm, and assured. Those who used the full set of CDs had faster recoveries than expected with less pain. There is information included in each set as to how to use the CDs and instructions for hospital personnel.[5]

[1]Rider, Mark. "Entrainment mechanisms are Involved in Pain Reduction, Muscle Relaxation and Music-mediated Imagery." *Journal of Music Therapy* XXII (4), pp.183-192. 1985.
[2]Jonas, Suzanne. *Pain Control.* 1990. available from www.InnerHarmonyHealthCenter.com
[3]Rider, Mark. "Treating Chronic Disease and Pain with Music Mediated Imagery. *Arts in Psychotherapy* Vol 14. pp113-120. 1987.
[4]"In ethereal harp music, hope for ailing hearts." AP wire story. 3/06.
[5]available at www.InnerHarmonyHealthCenter.com

CHAPTER 9

APPLICATIONS OF MUSIC IN HOSPITAL UNITS, GERIATRICS, AND HOSPICE

For those who do not love, music drives away hate.
Music gives peace to the restless, and comforts the sorrowful.
They who no longer know where to turn find new ways,
And those who have despaired gain new confidence and love.
Pablo Casals, Cellist

Every unit in a hospital can benefit by the addition of music. It is important for practitioners to pay heed, though, to the prescriptiveness of music when applied in a particular setting. The following are examples of MusicMedicine in a variety of hospital units.

A beautiful and effect set of environmental music programs comes from MusiCure in Denmark. The music is based on more than seven years of research into the stimulating effect of specially designed music on hospitalized patients. Composed by Niels Eje in collaboration with leading doctors and nurses from "Musica Humana", the music is both physically relaxing and comforting, and can also provide mental stimulation for the patient when listened to through headphones. I play these CDs in my clinic waiting area and people always comment on how lovely and relaxing the music is. Because of the research and scientific documentation behind the creation of MusiCure, the CDs are only available at pharmacies in Denmark and Norway, and through Gefion Records at www.MusiCure.com.

GENERAL HOSPITAL UNITS
Hospital Entrance
There is not a room or area of the hospital that cannot benefit from the addition of *appropriate* music, starting at the entrance. People

coming into a hospital are nervous if not fearful. A hospital is one place no one really wants to be. Many hospitals have musicians donating some time to play for visitors; this gives a welcoming feeling. As you might expect, either calm music or familiar popular songs are most appreciated. MusiCure CDs would be most appropriate here.

Emergency Waiting Room

This is another area where no one wants to be! Music has been used successfully in the areas of emergency rooms; light orchestral music that is soothing and peaceful in nature is favored. People have reported being less scared and more relaxed. Some of the current New Age music or the *SO Chord** might also be appropriate here (see Appendix A for suggestions). For children, separate headphones and tape players with children's familiar songs or stories are a great assist in calming.

Radiation Treatments/X-Ray

Positive results happen when music is playing while patients undergo radiation treatments. The patients feel more relaxed as the music distracts from the coldness and emptiness of the room. Quiet music playing in the X-Ray waiting room is also helpful. See the recommendations in Appendix A under Relaxation/Stress Reduction.

MRI/CAT Scan

Many patients exhibit significant fear and anxiety at having to be placed in the coffin-like equipment for an MRI. Patients who took a personal audio player and music with them reported a decrease in their anxiety and an ability to keep their thoughts on something pleasant. In this situation personal preference or a guided imagery CD would be suggested.

Intensive Care/Coronary Care Units (ICU/CCU)

In the ICU and CCU, music has been found to lower the incidence of heart attacks and other heart complications, to decrease heart rate, increase tolerance for pain and suffering, lessen anxiety and depression, increase energy, and decrease insomnia. I have sometimes witnessed dramatic changes in patients who were given a prescriptive course of music/sound therapy (see Appendix A).

For the music to be successful, a regimen of listening must be established. Keep thinking of this as *Music Medicine*, so respect and honor a routine or your results will be sporadic. Examples include:

~ Listen to a relaxation tape 3 times a day for 1/2 hour prior to a procedure.
~Use an insomnia tape every night at a specified hour and if the patient wakes during the night.
~Use preferred music during painful procedures (see Chapter 8 for further routines).
~Alternate soothing classical music and Hemi-Sync Meta Music with a guided healing tape throughout the day.

I have found the use of a Hemi-Sync relaxation CD, *Relaxation/Self Healing** (by this author) highly effective in preparing patients to be weaned from ventilators. When the process of weaning does begin, switch to another Hemi-Sync CD, *H+Lung Repairs** (also use 3x/day), which gives the patient a self-suggestion to breathe easy whenever anxiety arises.

For CCU patients, I have found the guided imagery CD *Cardiac Healing** and the frequency CD *Oxygenator*,* alternated with music CDs, effective in strengthening the pulse and entraining irregular heart rates. Waltzes and music with a healthy heartbeat added (in some of the music for newborns) are most effective. For overall assistance in these units, I continue to have good results with the combination of Hemi-Sync *Relaxation/Self Healing** and *Blessings**. Two dramatic cases were described in Chapter 6 where using the *right* choice of music resulted in wonderful unexpected healings.

The question of patient preference between classical or popular music is an ongoing debate in selecting music for healing. While sedative music can slow heart rate and blood pressure and bring about a relaxation response, music therapy researcher Helen Bonny[1] found that patients in ICU who have acute and severe physical and emotional distress are less tolerant of music they would normally listen to in their daily lives, Classical music is the exception, which is more likely to contain elements that touch our souls and stimulate healing. In times when we are severely out of tune, we intuitively prefer to hear music that is soul filled and healing in nature.

In his work, Dr. Ary Goldberger of Harvard Medical School shows that varied rhythms created by healthy hearts are similar to note patterns in certain classical music. Dr. Mark Tramo, a Massachusetts General Hospital neurologist said parts of the brain involved in controlling emotions and reward-seeking behavior can have a profound influence on the heart. Music's influence on that part of the brain may explain how it can affect the heart.[2]

Former <u>coma</u> patients have described their experience several ways: as suspended animation, confusion, weird dreamlike perceptions, or no memory at all of the time that transpired. Many of these patients, though, are able to recall activities and people who were around them at various times in the hospital. Those coma patients who were read to from their favorite books or were played their favorite music often remember, and thank the people who did so once out of the coma. In one study David Aldridge[3], a music therapist, improvised wordless singing based on the tempo of the patient's pulse and breathing pattern. When any reaction on the part of the patient was observed, the phrase was repeated. When the therapist first began to sing, there was a slowing down of the heart rate. Then the heart rate rose rapidly and sustained an elevated level until the end of contact, approximately ten minutes. The patient's EEG measurement showed a desynchronization from theta rhythm to alpha or beta; there were grabbing movements of the hands and turning of the head. Her eyes opened and she returned to consciousness.

Effects of Music in Medical Treatment

Intensive Care

    Physiological

                                      less pain medications needed
decrease in heart rate
decrease in blood pressure
fewer medical complications
improved respiration
reduced myocardial infarction rate
decreased mortality rate

    Psychological   improved mood

    Psychophysiological reduced anxiety

Pulmonology

    Physiological   improved airway resistance
increased forced expiratory flow
increased forced vital capacity
increased peak expiratory flow
reduction in respiration rate
less heart rate increase
easier transitions from ventilators

    Psychophysiological reduced anxiety

Table 3.

Cancer Units

Many journal articles have addressed the use of music with cancer patients to relieve pain and suffering, promote relaxation, and reduce anxiety. Since symptoms in the cancer patient are of a biopsychosocial nature, the use of music is particularly helpful because of music's ability to cut across barriers. Significant uses of music therapy in this area are summarized in Table 4. (Munro & Mount[4], and others)

Music may be successfully administered by individuals not formally trained in Music Medicine, however, the professionally trained music therapist bases her interventions on a thorough knowledge of all facets of music, and a broad awareness of the behavioral sciences, treatment and education models, and accepted therapeutic approaches. The Pain Service at Memorial Sloan-Kettering Cancer Center in NY City has developed a collaborative approach to patients that includes a music therapist along with a psychiatrist, nurse clinician, neuro-oncologist, chaplain, and social worker. Music therapy in this model is used to promote relaxation, reduce anxiety, supplement other pain control methods, and enhance communication between patient and family[5]. It is clear that the approach of music therapy with cancer patients can address more of the healing process than simply the reduction of physical symptoms.

Sound therapy has also been used effectively in treating cancer with the application of specific frequencies assessed through Voice Spectral Analysis. (See BioAcoustics in Chapter 7). This entails an individual session with a trained therapist to assess which frequencies are most beneficial for this patient.

Music in the Treatment of Cancer

Physical	promotes muscular relaxation breaks the cycle of chronic pain decreases side effects of chemotherapy decreases nausea and vomiting facilitates physical participation in activities
Psychological	reinforces identity and self-concept improves mood decreases anxiety and depression assists in recall of significant past events assists in expression of both conscious and unconscious feelings reinforces reality aids the expression of fantasy and imagination effects a direct appeal to the emotions.

Social	provides a means of socially acceptable self-
	expression
	provides a bridge across cultural differences
	           and isolation
	provides a bond and sense of community with
	           family members
	provides a link to life before the illness
	provides an opportunity to participate in a group
	provides entertainment and diversion

Spiritual	assists the expression of spiritual feelings
	stimulates feelings of comfort and reassurance
	provides an avenue for expressing doubts, anger,
	           fear of punishment, and questions on the
	           ultimate reality of life.

Table 4.

Much research demonstrates the benefits of oxygen therapy. The *Oxygenator** CD contains the frequencies of oxygen (plus other frequencies) for a direct delivery into the body. There is no concern for over-oxygenating the body as it will absorb only what it needs.

The work of Fabian Maman[6] is also very exciting. His studies show the destabilization and explosion of Hela cancer cells under the influence of certain notes. Attaching an ordinary camera to a microscope, he played various instruments near the cells. He observed that when only one sound with one type of impulse and only one level of energy was emitted, "the Hela cell seemed better able to accommodate itself and perhaps to balance itself and keep its structure longer." When the human voice was used singing the C scale, the greatest effect occurred. Within 9 minutes the cells enlarged, destabilized and exploded. In later studies using Kirilian photography he found the greatest resonance between cell and voice, i.e. the most change, when the person sang to her own cells. A sound therapist's prescription would definitely include singing and toning to influence the cells.

Surgery - see Chapter 8

Pediatrics

Pediatrics was one of the very first areas to discover the effectiveness of the record player and familiar music in providing pleasure and simplifying custodial care. Nurses have freely added their own talents as music makers, singing a variety of familiar songs (even TV commercials) with encouraging results. Children's responses to familiar music are both immediate and long term. "Music provides a release of angry tension, some satisfaction of their human need for warmth and friendliness, and lessened feelings of isolation. Music involves the individual so totally and in such a unique fashion that closeness is felt, and painful aloneness may be alleviated...Music is nearly always an expression of good will, a reaching out to others"[7]. Because reaching out encourages a reciprocal response, music promotes relating to others. Anxious, fearful and angry children are able to express pleasure and rhythm, to grow to accept other patients and caretakers, and to become involved with others through group music making.

I remember one four-year old child with leukemia who was in the hospital for chemotherapy. I will call her Lisa. Lisa would not talk or interact with anyone but her parents, one of whom was at the hospital at all times. One day, I invited her and her father into the empty playroom, where I gave her a drum and a tambourine and I began singing "this Old Man." Lisa would occasionally beat the drum or participate with the hand motions of the song. As I became 'silly', she began to smile and participate more. Soon other small children came into the playroom and became part of our singing group with rhythm instruments. Lisa still did not sing, but became the conductor for our songs and even whispered suggestions of what to sing in my ear. Soon all the ambulatory children, some parents, and all the staff were participating in our group. Smiles were everywhere and the feeling of joy was contagious. After that experience, Lisa would interact with others, smile, and bring her parents to the playroom. She left the hospital without having verbally expressed herself to anyone, but she was visibly happier.

In another hospital, amazing results occurred during the biweekly visits of the "Music Man" to the pediatric ward. "Children, staff, and parents quickly came to recognize and welcome the soft sounds that [brought] a brief respite from the anxieties and tensions of hospital life"[8]. He was dressed as the Pied Piper, with interesting instruments, ribbons and cords dangling from his person--silver bells, slide whistle, guitar, recorder, kazoo, tambourine, and castanets. He would use the slide whistle to make initial contact with distressed or distracted children, and silver bells with the listless ones. Once he had their attention, he began to play and sing familiar songs.

Infants and Toddlers

The same results can be obtained with this preverbal population. Music's nonverbal communication quickly establishes rapport, with the results that crying and frustrating behavior are reduced, calm or sleep can be induced, and socialization promoted. When we prescribe specific music for various age groups, the most dramatic results come from infants who hear a human heartbeat followed by music or a recording of the mother's voice. I have seen babies immediately stop crying and fall asleep as if the sound was the cue they had been waiting for.

Effects of Music in Medical Treatment	
Neonatology	
Physiological	more rapid weight gain
	increased food acceptance
	reduced vomiting and gagging
	increased oxygen saturation levels
	shorter hospital stay
Behavioral	reduced crying
	improved behavioral states
Pediatrics	
Psychological	increased verbalizations regarding illness
	help families adjust to child's illness
	improved mood
	decreased fear
Behavioral	decreased behavioral distress
Psychophysiological	decreased anxiety
	decreased pain
	reduction in stress symptoms

Tab;e 5.

Burn Centers

Children in burn centers are more cooperative during painful moves when they are simultaneously singing action songs, and more relaxed during hydrotherapy while listening to slow music and engaged in guided imagery. They experience shorter periods of delirium when familiar songs with strong repeated rhythms and cadences are played. The predictability and familiarity allow caregivers to maintain contact with the child. In this context it is strongly recommended that music be administered by a music therapist. The relationship with the music therapist, who is not associated with painful procedures, has been found to be more relaxing. The therapist can also be instrumental in building up both the psychological strength to cope and the patient's self esteem. This can be achieved through song writing, learning how to play an instrument, and performance.

Asthma

Asthmatic children have also gained self-esteem from music therapy during their hospital stays. In this program, active participation in rhythm games, singing playing wind instruments, and movement to music builds endurance, develops muscle strength, and improves posture and breath control. Listening to soothing music regulates breathing patterns and relieves anxiety. (See Appendix A for further recommendations for children.) Adults with asthma respond very well to the Hemi-Sync CD *Lung Repairs and Maintenance** which teaches a code word to say when airways begin to constrict. I would also recommend listening to *Oxygenator**, a CD of specific frequencies to increase the amount of oxygen in the body. It is also highly effective in relieving the congestion brought upon by colds.

GERIATRICS

In nursing homes, music is used to affect mind, body, emotions, and spirit. As part of the patient intake information, it is important and useful to find out what the patient's favorite music preferences are so appropriate music can be used. In what is often the highlight of their day, patients come together to sing, move, reminisce, and ease physical and emotional pain. Even patients who tend to sit quietly all day respond to music of their generation, i.e., popular songs from when they were ages 18-25. Most join in and sing the words even if the actual program is not singing but movement exercise. Smiles erupt and memories are shared. Other favorites are folk songs and spirituals. *Amazing Grace* is one song with almost universal appeal.

The goals of music as geriatric therapy are many: to reinforce occupational and physical therapy goals and increase range of motion; to motivate socialization, and to enhance behavioral re-patterning and reality orientation. To elicit these powerful responses, the music must have meaning and significance to the individual. Music selections should be discussed with the patient's family to avoid music that evokes very unpleasant memories in the patient.

In this setting, music is not a luxury but a necessity, as the music can substitute some of what their brains or bodies no longer provide. In 1991, physicians, music therapists, and patients in support of music therapy testified before the United States Congress Senate Special Committee on Aging. The National Association for Music Therapy (now the American Music Therapy Association) urged Congress to allocate a modest amount of "special projects" money for the research and publication of music therapy strategies for individuals suffering from Alzheimer's disease and various other forms of dementia, stroke, depression, grief, and other disabling conditions. They pointed out that the efficacy of music therapy has been demonstrated through extensive clinical practice, but demonstration projects, basic research, and clinical outcome research could extend and further validate music therapy applications. The Administration on Aging then awarded twelve grants for music therapy projects. This was an astounding and historic advance in the provision of music therapy services for vulnerable elderly people.

Altzheimer's Disease

Much anecdotal evidence has accrued regarding the effects of music on patients with Alzheimer's. It apparently stimulates the mind in a way that allows easier expression of moods and personality, more orderly thought structure, and more reliable memory retrieval. Caregivers have noted increased communication, group cohesion, rhythmic movement and touching behaviors when music is played. A 1997 study demonstrated these effects. Lind Institute's *Adagio* and *Largo** tapes were selected to initially reduce the verbal and physical agitation during meals. Not only did the amount of agitation decrease 59%, but the patients attempted to socialize with one another, touch one another, and stay after meals to listen to the music. Mozart sonatas also assist these patients in focusing and attention.

Playing the patient's favorite music has shown to be an important avenue for one-on-one communication. Patients will generally focus on the music and attempt to share old memories or feelings with whoever is present. It is an especially successful treatment in family groups who have lost communication with their loved one.

Live music is a wonderful stimulator for these patients. Having a musician/singer perform "old standards" generally elicits responses in the form of singing, clapping, smiling, socializing, touching. Many normally nonverbal patients will engage in singing or using rhythm instruments during live sing-a-longs.

THE TERMINALLY ILL/HOSPICE

Music's holistic attributes are of great value with patients who are terminally ill. Patients use the music to air their negative feelings and release emotions associated with their prognosis, to help them move through the stages of anger to acceptance. Music also becomes a bridge to the past to help recall and acknowledge old memories as well as to heighten awareness of participation in the present. Music can stimulate discussions on religion and life after death. It can forge connection between the conscious world, the various levels of the subconscious, and the transpersonal. (See the discussion of guided imagery and music [GIM] in Chapter 4.) Music can ease the death struggle of the terminally ill. One trained GIM nurse played specific GIM tapes for three restless patients during their last hours of life. She observed in two of the three patients a noticeable calming during the second tape, appropriately titled "Transitions". In both cases, a quiet passing from this life ensued shortly thereafter. In my own experience playing the patient's favorite music or quiet "spiritual" (as in *Largo**, *Classical Interlude**) music during the final hours casts a quiet, calming spell in the room that assists both the family and patient to let go and find resolution and peace. (Other appropriate music is listed in Appendix A under "Soul Music".)

When working with hospice or terminally ill persons, it is helpful to obtain a music history either from them or their family.

Questions to ask are:

    Were they a musician?
    Do they like to sing?
    What are their listening preferences?
    Did they attend concerts?
    Did they take music lessons?
    What was their childhood experience with music?
    What is their cultural background?

Some possible activities are:

    Concert going
    Instrument playing; lessons

Drawing/painting to music
Song or poetry writing
Sharing favorite recordings with family/friends

When using music for symptom reduction, **PRESENTATION IS EVERYTHING!**

~ Ask the patient "What are your needs? What would you like?"

~Determine the symptoms to be managed or results desired. (See MT Checklist in Appendix D for assistance in this process.)

~Be encouraging. Patients will try CDs if you are 'sold' on them.

~Know your CDs before recommending them--describe the CD and possible benefits.

~Use headphones if possible, or flat speaker that fits under the pillow. (See Appendix B)

~Monitor vital signs if possible (before, during, after).

~Follow up is VERY important--encourage discussion of the experience.

The Chalice of Repose Project, founded by Therese Schroeder-Sheker, is an initiative in which deaths in homes, hospitals, and hospices are eased by music offered by highly trained individuals or teams. Their work is called "musical-sacramental-midwifery." A musician plays and/or sings specific music for conscious patients, other music for those who are comatose, those in physical pain, mental agony, etc. "The new midwife is a chalice, and sings with bright longing for the simultaneous reception of spirit and matter, humanity and divinity.... A conscious, blessed death changes everyone involved.... Together, the living and the dying form choirs of celebrants who bridge the two worlds by dissolving and creating themselves in the mystical body of Christ or the rainbow body of Buddhism." [9]

*Available from www.InnerHarmonyHealthCenter.com

[1]Bonny, Helen. *Music Rx.* Port Townsend, WA: ICM West. 1982.
[2]"In ethereal harp music, hope for ailing hearts". AP wire service, 3/06.
[3]Aldridge, David. "Where Am I? – Music Therapy Applied to Coma Patients." *Journal of Royal Society of Medicine._* V.83, June 1990.
[4]Munro, S., Mount, B. "Music Therapy in Palliative Care". *Canadian Medicine Assoc., Journal* 119 (9): 1029-1034.
[5]Coyle, Nessa. A Model of Continuity of Care for Cancer Patients with Chronic Pain". *Medical Clinics of North America,* Vol 71 No. 2, March 1987.
[6]Mamon, Fabian. *The Role of Music in the 21st Century.* Tama-Do Press, 1997.
[7]Gaston, E. Thayer (Ed). *Music in Therapy._* N.Y.: MacMillan. 1968.
[8]Lindsay, K.E. "The value of Music for Hospitalized Infants." *Children's Health care:* 9(4), 104-107. 1981.
[9]Schroeder-Sheker, Therese. Musical-Sacramental-Midwifery: The Use of Music in Death and Dying. In *Music & Miracles,* Don Campbell. Quest Books, Wheaton, Il. 1992.

CHAPTER 10

APPLICATIONS OF MUSIC IN REHABILITATION

Imagine a form of therapy which benefits nearly every user in terms of increased vitality, renewed motor skills, increased mobility, and easing of pain.
Imagine, too, that it is able to reach some patients whose physical condition isolates and immobilizes them....
Then imagine it costs almost nothing....
and that is just what music therapists [are doing].
Journal of American Medical Association, 9/11/91

Adults require inpatient rehabilitative therapy for a variety of conditions, including stroke, rheumatoid arthritis, MS, prolonged hospital-stay deterioration, amputation, spinal cord or head injury. They can range in ages from 18-95, and receive a regimen of treatments to facilitate their independence. These treatment modalities may include a psychological evaluation and adjustment counseling; physical, occupational, and speech therapies; medication; and optimally, recreational and music therapy.

Music therapy is increasingly being utilized in physical rehabilitation programs. As health care organizations place more emphasis on the patients' functional independence in life activities, it has been shown that music therapy can address the functional needs of this population in the areas of cognition, communication, physical functioning, activities of daily living, and psychosocial functioning. According to the Joint Commission on Accreditation of Healthcare Organizations[1], the range of services offered in physical rehabilitation programs may include but is not limited to the following: "audiology, creative arts therapies, dental, dietetic, educational, occupational therapy, physical therapy, prosthetic and/or orthotic, psychological, recreational therapy, rehabilitation engineering, rehabilitation medicine, rehabilitation nursing, social work, speech-language pathology, and vocational rehabilitation services."

The tremendous value of music is its ability to simultaneously influence mind, body, spirit, and emotions. Used regularly, like any prescribed medication, music is an effective outlet for feelings of stress; an assistant in clarifying issues; decreasing symptoms and increasing the body's own healing mechanisms. And music that touches our spirits can assist us in both transcending and transforming emotional and physical suffering.

BASIC MUSICMEDICINE INTERVENTIONS IN PHYSICAL REHABILIATION UNITS

By adhering to the following considerations and recommendations, basic musicmedicine can be implemented with success by conscientious nurses and therapists. The first and most important step is to decide on the purpose of the application of music/sound: what does one want the music/sound to do for the patient? Then consider the variables in success: the presentation; assessment of patient's mental, physical, and listening states as outlined in Chapter 5; appropriate recommendation; and **consistency**. A Music Therapy Check List to assist in this process is included in Appendix D.

Presentation of Musical Medicine

For successful intervention, music tapes/CDs must be presented as an important part of the patient's treatment and given the same weight as taking medications. Therefore, the implementer must present the therapy in a convincing and structured way. For example, "I recommend (or Dr. so and so recommends) the use of specific music/sound to assist in decreasing your pain so you don't have to rely on medications. This is a successful intervention and promoted by our unit. You will be listening to this tape three times a day. We will help you and try to keep you from being disturbed while you listen. I think now is a good time to start." There are several points to keep in mind: 1) be positive; 2) show firm belief in the modality; 3) be directive--don't ask what they think about it; (remember, to be effective musical medicine should be thought of as a medication) 4) promote the positive outcome of self control and decreasing chemicals; and 5) help the patient in carrying out the schedule, i.e. assist with the tape player, and DO NOT INTERRUPT the patient when she is listening.

118

BODY
The Relaxation Response

We are endowed with two gross, innate, biobehavioral responses: the stress response and the relaxation response, that are in direct contrast to one another. "The stress response is characterized physiologically by increased heart rate and blood pressure and by the narrowing of blood vessels and catecholamine release; emotionally, by the subjective experiences of discomfort, fear, and rage; and biosocially, by the flight-fight response." As defined by Dr. Herbert Benson[2], the leading researcher on this effect, the relaxation response "is a reduction in the activity of the sympathetic nervous system...that brings on bodily changes that decrease heart rate, lowers metabolism, decrease the rate of breathing, and bring the body back into a health[y] balance"; emotionally, by subjective experiences of comfort and trust along with receptivity to new information; and biosocially, by an increased capacity for social interaction and bonding." The relaxation response has been found to be one of the key variables in a person's ability to heal. Music has been shown to help us achieve the relaxation response.

Symptom Reduction

Symptom Reduction addresses some of the same psycho/physiological symptoms so readily treated with medications. As a result of modern technology and decades of research determining music's affect on symptoms, specific recommendations are given in Table 6 at the end of this chapter and in other chapters of this book. The CDs recommended are a result of my work in a rehabilitation center and have been found to be highly successful. The importance of listening on an established schedule cannot be stressed too often. This assists in establishing new patterns in the body. As an example, an anxiety music program should include listening to tapes at least three times per day, whether or not the patient is feeling increased anxiety; insomnia tapes MUST be listened to every night. When the programs are faithfully followed, not only are patients able to learn some control over their own functioning, but the need for medications are decreased, other therapies are performed more easily and successfully, and the patient's own sense of hopefulness and control increases.

Pain Reduction - see discussion in Chapter 8

Physical Therapy

There are an increasing number of studies demonstrating the effect of music on one's motor system[3]. Music serves to increase the general mobility, muscular strength and coordination, gait and balance, and social interaction of patients. They are able not only to increase their range of motion while listening to music, but also to increase their tolerance for repetition. It is the rhythmic element of music that has been noted to override poorly established motor patterns. An innovative study from Colorado State University studied rhythmic auditory stimulation with stroke patients. Metronome pulses were embedded in music that was listened to through headphones. Patients showed improved cadence, stride, and foot placement with lasting effects. It appears that the beat excites and shapes activity in the motor system of the brain that helps organize and integrate complex movement. In this therapy, it is not music's emotional or motivational value but the entrainment effect upon movement frequencies.

There are several factors to consider when implementing music in Physical Therapy[4]:

1. Given the complexity of neuromuscular and skeletal disorders, a therapist needs to be careful in operationally defining the areas to be changed then develop and select the appropriate activities and music. (Decide what you want the music to do.)

2. Patients respond best to familiar tunes with which they can identify.

3. Simple music, with a clear and distinctive beat and rhythmic pattern, is essential.

4. The tempo of the music is crucial: it must match the activity, e.g., for side-to-side weight shifting in a sitting, position use music of 58-63 beats per minute (bpm). Patients who are comfortable with the tempo (not too fast), will strain less.

5. Music should suit the desired movement, e.g., stretch movements require flowing melodies, while foot tapping requires a heavier, more punctuated orchestration.

6. Each new pattern of movement should be rehearsed prior to its performance with music; some verbal cueing is necessary from the therapist throughout the session.

7. Group sessions demonstrate the greatest gains in both physical and social interaction between participants. Familiar music stimulates spontaneous singing, whistling, or humming and decreases anxiety. Opportunities to reach and touch another appears to be very

beneficial, i.e., patients sit in a circle close enough for them to touch one another and perform goal-oriented movements of reaching to touch a neighbor's shoulder, knee, hands or feet.

Dance in a group format has also been used with a variety of physical disabilities, including leg amputation, stroke, and rheumatoid arthritis. The patients significantly increased their enjoyment of exercise and rest, as well as improving their scores in range of motion.[5]

The Stroke Recovery Series* of Hemi-Sync tapes contains several tapes to that support exercise. The tapes are to be listened to through headphones, lying down. The focus is on both sides of the body and imagining movements. I used these with several hemi-paresis patients in between PT and OT sessions. Although difficult to assess, the patients felt the exercises contributed to their recovery. These patients were noticeably less anxious during subsequent PT sessions and had more positive attitudes. The Monroe Institute has collected many case studies demonstrating the effectiveness of Hemi-Sync tapes with CVA patients[6]. Common themes of improvement were: increased feelings of relaxation; continued improvement even after two years; increased ability to image; and decrease of pain.

Occupational Therapy

Although there has been less research on music applied in this area, I have found music to be useful as background in the morning while patients are bathing and getting dressed. Lively, familiar music assisted in raising spirits and decreasing the time needed to perform these tasks.

Individual music making is also very useful in this therapy. If patients had played an instrument prior to their impairment, bringing their instrument to the OT session to assist in increasing range of motion and flexibility was proven successful. Playing rhythm instruments like maracas while listening to music also increases range of motion, once again demonstrating the importance of rhythmic stimulation on motor functioning.

MIND
Speech Therapy

Several studies demonstrate music's effectiveness in assisting organized, recognizable speech with traumatic brain-injured patients[7]. Aphasic patients with left hemisphere damage unable to produce normal speech are often able to sing their thoughts to familiar music. Melodic Intonation Therapy (MIT) is a treatment approach with aphasics that utilizes the client's unimpaired ability to sing to facilitate spontaneous and voluntary speech. Starting with the singing of short phrases to known melodies, the patient progresses to chanting sentences in more normal inflection patterns of speech.

In a study comparing the effects of singing and rhythmic interventions, singing has also been shown to increase verbal intelligibility and improve rate of speech in TBI patients. The use of a familiar melody was a key variable.

Background music during ST sessions can also facilitate a decrease in anxiety and increased focusing ability. Several suggestions are: Mozart's Symphonies #1-17, his flute sonatas, and Superlearning CDs. Superlearning[8] is a program that uses the research of Soviet-bloc scientists on the use of music in learning. Their results show that Baroque music (classical music from the 17th and early 18th centuries) creates a relaxed state that lowers blood pressure, synchronizes heartbeat and brain waves to slower, more efficient rhythms, and promotes hemisphericity, the synchronization of the right and left hemispheres. In this country, Ostrander and Schroeder[9] have incorporated these findings into tapes that use rhythm, breathing, and music of 60 beats per minute.

Several speech therapists with whom I have worked have tried the hemi-sync tape *Concentration** with notable results over a period of time. Played softly through headphones, the hemi-sync signals assisted in increasing attentiveness, organization, and short-term memory. Patients remarked how much easier it was to accomplish the tasks presented. The *Stroke Recovery Series** also contains some speech exercise tapes.

Music Therapy with Rancho Levels of Head Injury

In addition to the above, the uses of music and sound with head-injured patients include coordinating Rancho Levels with interventions[11]. Many former Level 1 coma patients are able to recall activities and people who were around them at various times in the hospital. Those coma patients who were read to from their favorite books or were played their favorite music often remember, and thank the people who did so. The general goal of assessment for the Level 11- and 11I-coma patient is to determine what kind of musical stimulus produces alerting or orienting responses. The stimulus is played for 10-15 seconds, followed by 30 seconds of silence. A verbal cue may be given to prepare the client. The stimuli should include as wide a variety of instrumental sounds as possible. Careful observations and recordings should be made to compare the data. In one study[12] a music therapist improvised wordless singing based on the tempo of the patient's pulse and breathing pattern. When any reaction on the part of the patient was observed, the phrase was repeated. When the therapist first began to sing, there was a slowing down of the heart rate. Then the heart rate rose rapidly and sustained an elevated level until the end of contact, approximately 10 minutes. The patients' EEG measurement showed a desynchronization from theta rhythm to alpha or beta; there were grabbing movements of the hand and turning of the head and then eyes opening to the return of consciousness.

Music therapy can also assist in increasing the client's awareness of the environment. One technique involves giving feedback about the client's behavior in song, i.e. improvise songs about clothing, random movements, weather, date, and time. Familiar songs about the season or day can also be sung. The use of music and hemi-sync music with in-patients is effective in calming and decreasing impulse control.

In Levels IV--VI, clients are given the opportunity to use strengths in addressing goals ranging from active responsiveness to following simple functional directives. A patient may respond with more accuracy to directives and questions that are sung rather than spoken[10]. For instance, Gervin[13] sang one and two stage commands, sung to familiar music, to traumatic brain injury patients during dressing to promote independence. The patients would sing in response, learning the sequential steps for dressing. This is much like the songs we sang as children to learn activities. This song technique has been found to be very successful with patients with left frontal lobe damage or bilateral damage.

Playing soothing, instrumental music with an even beat and tempo in the background gives the patient an alternate focus and quiet environment. Recommendations include *Largo** or *Baroque Gardens**, or *Harmonic Melodies*. Several hemi-sync CDs have been useful: *Cloudscapes**, *Midsummer Night**, and *Remembrance**.

Concussion

In my experience with outpatients who sustained concussions, Hemi-Sync tapes were highly effective in decreasing headaches, irritability, fatigue, sleeplessness and insomnia, anxiety, as well as improving concentration. I recommend *H+ Brain Repairs and Maintenance** and *Deep Relaxation**. The Monroe Institute also has a collection of case studies documenting improvements related to the listening of their tapes[14]. Common themes from these cases include: increased energy, concentration, verbal and written communication; decreased anxiety; and improvements even after six years.

EMOTIONS

Shamans, medicine men/women, and psychiatric personnel have utilized music, chanting, or drumming to create an atmosphere of heightened emotion in which to heal. In these situations, the music helps center one's attention on the ritual and intent and intensify the feelings of the participants. Many studies demonstrate music's ability to evoke memories, increase or decrease emotional states, and change moods. As the medical establishment refocuses on the importance of emotions in the healing process, the use of music is a natural adjunct to assist in decreasing anxiety and depression. A perfect example is the 75-year old widower who had suffered a mild left CVA with resulting right hemi-paresis. He was angry, belligerent, and uncooperative. He refused to take any tapes to listen to that evening until I made a deal with him to delay psychological testing. Even then, he would not choose a tape so I gave him a tape of love songs sung by Linda Rondstadt. The next morning when I came down the hall, his nurses immediately wanted to know what I had said to him and what was on the tape. Apparently he had listened to the music several times, wept, and slept peacefully, all without communicating with the staff. When he awoke he was a new man, cooperative, cheerful, and ready to fully participate in his rehabilitation program. When he came back to me to complete the battery of psychological tests he would only say that the tape was beautiful and how good it made him feel. He would disclose no more.

When people find themselves suddenly incapacitated AND hospitalized they experience a loss of control and a sense of helplessness that can quickly change to hopelessness and depression. In these situations music can be a constant companion and friend. It is important to allow patients to listen to their favorites be it opera, Big Band music, hymns, or show tunes; whatever they will willingly listen to will help. Patient after patient would begin to smile, relax, and in general feel better from listening to familiar music. They would also begin to talk about the music with each other, trade tapes, and improve socially. A nurse who was in one of my training programs called six months later to relate a story of her experience with an older man in her ICU unit who was belligerent and constantly on the call button for minute reasons. She stated up until this day she had been reluctant to try using music because she felt unsure of herself. But for some reason she asked the patient if he liked music. He began quite a long story of his involvement in music that led to her asking his family to bring in a CD player and music. From that day on he was more cooperative, smiled more, engaged in conversation, his presenting symptoms began to diminish, and, important for the nurses, left the call button alone. This nurse is now a total convert and approaches all of her patients with music medicine.

The addition of a live performer is also a bonus. Patients will sing, move, tap, clap, smile, hum, laugh, and cry and feel happier from the experience.

SPIRIT

When medical professionals and the public talk about mind/body health, the suggestion is that it is about gaining mental control of physical functions. Fine. But I have seen and heard of enough patients recovering from physical afflictions who did not consciously put their mind into physical gear to realize that healing is not a matter of mechanism. There is a part of us that transcends our humanness, a part that is wise: spirit. Our mentally identified culture has a tendency to deny mystery, to deny the spiritual. The Institute of Noetic Sciences has compiled a collection of thousands of well-documented cases of people who have recovered from an illness when all mental, medical, chemical means had been exhausted (www.InstituteofNoeticSciences.com). The cases are from various medical journals throughout the world and we can safely assume there are thousands more from medical practitioners that have not made it into the journals. I encountered many, one of which illustrates this point. When I first met 'Mary' she was 27 and admitted with unknown causes of multi-infarcts leaving her entire body weak with some right side paresis. The medical history that she related to me included the following. At 16 she was diagnosed with cervical cancer and her doctor started her on a six-week treatment of chemotherapy. At the end of the six weeks she felt worse, and the condition of the cancer had not changed; her physician recommended further chemotherapy. She felt hopeless and sick and elected not to continue the treatment. Her doctor told her to prepare to die and gave her no more than six months. She adopted an "I don't care attitude", got married, and set off on a trip across the US to explore her country. They did what they pleased, when they pleased, and had fun. Two years later, still alive, she returned to the same OB/GYN office to have a pregnancy test. Not only were they surprised to see her, they only found scar tissue in her cervix. As for her later hospital stay, no treatment or diagnosis was useful so she discharged herself and disappeared into the world.

What then is the spiritual? Dr. Rachel Naomi Remen[15] states it is not morals, ethics, the psychic, or religion. But it is recognition that there is something that is an essential part of human nature; there is something in all of us that seeks to connect with it. Certain pieces of music, largely classical, have the ability to connect with this inner self. The music is many sided and able to touch all parts of ourselves: mind, body, and emotions. It is healing music; it transcends our current condition. (More discussion on this in Chapter 6.) Appendix A contains several recommendations of music to use for this purpose under Soul Music.

IMAGERY

There are many researchers studying the effects of visualization on healing. Psychologist and researcher Jeanne Achterberg, while studying a group of terminally ill cancer patients, found that the most reliable way of predicting how they would fare against their disease was their mental imagery. This was more accurate even than immune component levels in the blood. Dr. Robert Trestman[16] has corroborated this study. In the arena of music therapy, an important psychological treatment is guided imagery and music developed by Dr. Helen Bonny[17], a music therapist. One of the most noticeable reactions to listening to music is the images that are evoked. They can be useful in understanding one's process, disease, emotions, and relationships. (Further discussion is in Chapter 3.)

One dramatic case comes to mind. An amputee patient, who was appropriately angry over her situation and experiencing significant phantom pain, was given a tape of specially programmed classical music to illicit imagery. The nurse prepared her by having her do some deep breathing and then telling her to imagine that she was in her

126

favorite place in nature. She then turned on the music (which was listened to through headphones) and made sure the patient would not be disturbed. When the nurse checked on her an hour later, the patient was calm and out of pain. She commented that the music took her out of the hospital, away from her pain and fears, and left her feeling peaceful. The patient asked to hear that tape several times; her behavior changed from resistant to motivated and she initiated socializing. Listening to image producing music can assist in transporting oneself out of the present resulting in decreases in anxiety, fear, pain, and boredom.

Imagery exercises focusing on specific areas of the body to increase healing are also extremely beneficial. I have had many patients who have been able to control pain and decrease other physical symptoms by the use of imagery.

SUMMARY

Music has tremendous value in medicine. It has the ability to simultaneously influence the mind, physiology, emotions, and spirit. Used regularly, like medications, music and sound are effective change agents to assist in our healing. The basic recommendations given in this chapter can be administered by staff, however, just like the nursing profession, professionally trained music therapists are the best ones to perform music therapy. The American Music Therapy Association is working very hard to have music therapy be included in third party reimbursements. If you have found music useful in your medical setting, please inform your insurance companies. This holistic, powerful medium needs to be included in everyone's healing protocol.

Table 6. Symptom Reduction (more suggestions in Appendix A)
*Most CDs are available through Music & Medicine at www.InnerHarmonyHealthCenter.com

Symptom	Music Components	Suggested CD	Listening Routine
Anxiety/Hypertension	soft, calm , consonant,	patient's choice	daily +PRN
	simple melodies	*Largo, Classical Interludes*	daily +PRN
	low pitched instruments	*So Chord* or *Unity*	daily +PRN
		Cloudscapes	daily
		Balance	PRN
	guided relaxation	Hemi-Sync: *Deep Relaxation*	3x/day
		H+ Relax	3x/day
		Jonas: *Color Relax/The Beach*	3x/day
Bladder Function	any music with strong flowing water sounds	Dexter & Gordon: *Secret Fountain*	PRN
Cardiac Distress	calm, even rhythms	Strauss waltzes	PRN
		Chopin waltzes	
		guided imagery	
		Jonas: *Cardiac Healing, Forgiveness*	2x/day
	frequencies	music with added heartbeat *Oxygenator, DNA/RNA*	as much as possible
Depression	lively, fun, recognizable	patient's choice	PRN
		hymns, Big Band music	PRN
	imagery producing	Jonas: *Blessings, Forgiveness,*	1x/day +PRN
		Meeting Your Spirit Guide	
Insomnia	slow, quiet,	Rachmaninoff: *Vespers*	Nightly
		Weber: *Lullaby*	Nightly
		Hemi-Sync: *So Chord,*	Nightly
		Sleeping thru the Rain, Cloudscapes	
	guided relaxation	*Blessings; Color Relax*	
	Hemi-Sync:	*Sound Sleeper*	Nightly
		Super Sleep	Nightly
Pain	attention grabbing	patient's choice	PRN
	guided relaxation	*Color Relax/The Beach*	Daily
		Pain Control	Daily
		Hemi-Sync: *Deep Relaxation*	2x/day
		Energy Walk	2x/day
	frequencies	*Muscle Ease, Spinal Ease*	3-4x/day
Respiratory Distress	calm	*So Chord*	Daily
	guided relaxation	Hemi-Sync: *Deep Relaxation*	3x/day
		H+ Lung Repairs	3x/day
	frequencies	*Oxygenator*	as much as possible

128

[1]Joint Commission on Accreditation of Healthcare Organizations. *Accreditation manual for hospitals.* Oakbrook Terrace, IL, 1992.

[2]Benson, Herbert. *The Relaxation Response.* N.Y.: Avon Books, 1975.

[3]Staum, MJ. " Music for physical rehabilitation: Analysis of literature from 1950-1993 and applications for rehabilitation setting". In: Furman, CE, ed. *Effectiveness of Music Therapy Procedures: Documentation of research and clinical practice.* Washington, DC: National Association for Music Therapy, 1988:65-104.

[4]Cross, Patricia et al. "Observations on the use of music in rehabilitation of stroke patients *". Physiotherapy Canada* 1984; 36(4):197-201.

[5].____"Leaving the concert hall for clinic, therapists now test music's 'charms'". *JAMA* 1996; January 24/31, 275: 267-268.

[6] The Monroe Institute. Stroke recovery: case study reports. Faber, VA: The Monroe Institute,1996.

[7]Adamek, Mary, and Shiraishi, Iris. "Music therapy with traumatic brain-injured patients: speech rehabilitation, intervention models, and assessment procedures (1970-1995"). In, Furman, Charles, ed. *Effectiveness of music therapy procedures: Documentation of research and clinical practice.* Silver Spring, MD: National Association for Music Therapy, 1996: 267-279.

[8] www.Superlearning.com

[9] Ostrander, Sheila and Schroeder, Lynn. *Superlearning.* 1979.

[10].Claeys, Susan. "The Role of music and music therapy in the rehabilitation of traumatically brain-injured clients" In, Harvey, Arthur, ed. *Music and Health.* Louisville, KY: Music for Health Services Foundation, Eastern Kentucky University, 1988: 118-139.

[11]Claeys, MS, Miller, AC, Dalloul-Pampersad, R, & Kollar, M. "The role of music and music therapy in the rehabilitation of traumatically brain injured clients". *Music Therapy Perspectives* 1989; 6: 71-77.

[12]Adridge, David. "Where am I - music therapy applied to coma patients." *Journal of Royal Society of Medicine 6/90;83.*

[13]Gervin, AP. "Music therapy compensatory technique utilizing song lyrics during dressing to promote independence in the patient with a brain injury." *Music Therapy Perspectives* 1991; 9: 87-90.

[14] The Monroe Institute. *Brain injury: case study reports.* Faber, VA: The Monroe Institute, 1996.

[15]Remen, Rachel N. "Spirit: resource for healing". *Institute for Noetic Sciences Journal* 1988;Autumn: 5-9.

[16] Barasch, Marc Ian. *The Healing Path.* N.Y.: Penquin Books, 1994: 154-155.

[17]Bonny, Helen, and Savory, Louis. *Music and Your Mind.* N.Y.: Harper and Row, 1973

CODA

USING MUSIC IN YOUR EVERYDAY LIFE

Music hath charms to soothe the savage breast;
To soften rocks, or bend a knotted oak.
William Congreave, "The Mourning Bride"

All civilizations have recognized the power of music to heal, and the twentieth century's scientific investigations quantitatively prove what healers, shamans, medicine men/women, and our forefathers and mothers intuitively knew. Our response to musical experience is a matrix of elements--physical, emotional, cognitive, and spiritual. Table 7 shows all of the many ways music affects our Self.

How Music Effects Us			
MIND	**BODY**	**SPIRIT**	**EMOTIONS**
brain waves	pulse rate	socialization	anxiety
concentration	blood pressure	memories	fear
creativity	circulation	transpersonal	anger
aural center	muscular energy	imagery	depression
attention	respiration	ego	apprehension
synchronicity	GSR	id	loneliness
imagery	pupil size	superego	happiness
	ANS	patriotism	excitement
	pain		expression
	sleep		aura

Table 7.

One must always keep in mind the correct matching of a piece of music to the intended purpose for "music oft hath charms to make bad good, and good provoke to harm" (William Shakespeare). In choosing the *right* piece of music, ask first: **what do I want the music to do?** The general lists of music in this chapter match the qualities within the pieces of music to the desired outcome, and are intended to give you an overall picture of how to select music for use in your every day life to be healthier, happier, and more productive.

Starting Your Day One of the absolute worst ways to start the day is listening to the news. You have been, hopefully, sleeping peacefully and then you bombard your consciousness with tales of woe, death, and destruction, most of which you have no control over and will just raise your blood pressure. Try starting your day with some music. If you have a programmable CD alarm clock have music set to play that is 72 bpm, which will bring your heart rate up to normal and gently wake you. If you find that too soothing, pick music with a faster tempo, something you enjoy hearing. This might take a few mornings to find the most appropriate piece, and it will probably change over time. Have music on while dressing and eating breakfast. An aside, to fully start your day on the best note, eliminate sugar, caffeine, and processed foods from breakfast. Better choices are fruit, whole grains, eggs, a good quality multiple vitamin/mineral and probably an extra B complex and time release C. And one more thing that will help get your day off to a good start: give yourself enough time!

Drive to Work/School   If you live in a big city you might want to check the local traffic control station, but otherwise keep yourself in a positive mood by listening to music, OR, this is a great time to sing and tone. Toning is one of the best ways to get your body to vibrate and back into balance. Pick any note to tone, whichever one you pick will be the right one. Now, on that tone sing: ma   may   me   mo   moo…..slowly. Take deep breaths. You might find that you want to slide up or down. Remember, whatever you feel like doing is what you need now, so just do it. If you are driving kids to school, sing with them.   I have such great memories of driving in the car with my grandmother because she would sing all these old songs from her youth that had choruses we could all join in on.

Work/School   Music that appeals to the mind stimulates creativity and cognition, and assists with sustaining mental efforts. (More suggestions are in Appendix A under Cognitive Work, and Creativity).

Factory type work – use functional music, i.e., music that is programmed to your body cycles. Take into account the 'slump times' that occur every 1½ hours: the music should increase in tempo during those times. The tempo of the music should be 72 bpm to keep an even flow; familiar melodies help.

Computer/typing – music with a constant tempo that matches the rhythm/speed of the typist; Baroque music is most effective.

Creativity – to stimulate creativity use music that has some movement in melody, harmony, and rhythm but without abrupt changes, particularly in the tempo. Try imagery producing music to stimulate inspiration; but use environmental sounds CDs as background for artistic endeavors such as painting.

Cognitive Work/Studying – ordered, rhythmic, melodic music played on flute, violin as solo with orchestra, or piano works well. Have a little variation in dynamics and tempo using music with 60-72 bpm.

Breaks – take a break every 1½ hours: this coincides with our body's ultradian rhythmic cycles. Stretch, walk around, bend, drink lots of water, eat some raw nuts, do a five-minute aerobic routine to lively music that matches your movements.

Lunch – Get away from your work area! Your body and mind need a change. Think of it as 'recharge' time: go for a walk, do stretches, eat a balanced meal, take deep breaths, tell jokes.

Exercise – Chronobiologists tell us that the best time to exercise is between 4-6pm, when our bodies have been 'idle' and minds perhaps are overworked. Doing large motor exercise at this time re-oxygenates our blood which enriches our tissues, both body and mind. It also encourages maximum muscle recruitment. When doing any type of exercise, it is important that you match the tempo of the music with the tempo of your activity. For example, if you are walking or running, find music that matches your speed, where you are walking in sync with the beat. You will last longer and go farther.

Mood Alteration – Music is very helpful in establishing, enhancing, maintaining, and changing moods. For

Mood setting – use music of the desired mood as long as it is not too far from your present mood. (See the Mood Wheel in Chapter 3).

Mood alteration – use 'vectoring' as explained in Chapter 3, to match your mood, then gradually move to the mood desired as seen in the Mood Wheel.

Emotional release – play music that matches the mood you are in. If you are angry use energetic mood music (suggestions are in Appendix A) and let your anger out appropriately.

PreDinner – During this time you want lively music so it will stimulate your digestive juices. This is a good time for jazz or other pieces you like.

Dinner – During dinner, however, you want quiet, soothing music to assist with digestion and conversation. If you regularly experience digestive problems, try playing the *Digest Aid** CD in the background before, during, or after meals. Don't even think about eating in front of the TV or having it on in the background. As a matter of fact, kill your TV.

Massage – Sometime during the week give yourself the gift of a massage. Bring your own music that is slow and dreamy. If you are tense and overstressed, start with more lively music then change to slower music to assist in the unwinding process. *Illumination** CD is programmed to do this.

Meditation – There are several types of meditation practices, most of are effective in quieting the mind. When we are able to 'still' our minds, our bodies have an opportunity to heal, and we are able to be in touch with our intuition and higher sources of knowledge. Choose a style of meditation that works for you, one that you will practice. Mindfulness Meditation is an excellent choice for beginners, as is using a guided meditation CD like *Deep Relaxation** or *H+ Relax**. Intermediate and advanced meditators might like to try some of the recommended CDs in Appendix A.

Bedtime – Turn off the news. Do you really want to go into your dreamtime with conscious or unconscious thoughts of what you just heard? If you don't have any problems falling asleep, use a CD of quiet music or one of your frequency healing CDs. My favorites are: *Sleeping through the Rain*, Sonic Chakra Healer*, Oxygenator*, and Well Being**.

Insomnia – we all experience difficulty going to sleep at one time or another. Please don't reach for the sleeping pills. They will keep you from going into Delta state where your body recharges itself. Instead, try these tips:

1. Take a warm bath or shower with lavender essential oil.

2. Write about everything that you are worrying about. It will go from your mind to the paper. When you are finished writing, tell yourself your worries are safe and you won't forget them because they are all written down. When you lay your head down, ask your dreams for some creative solutions.

3. Put a few drops of lavender essential oil on your pillow and in your hands. Now breathe in the oil.

4. Imagine yourself in your favorite place in nature or at a vacation spot you particularly enjoyed.

5. There are two Hemi-sync CDs that are quite effective for insomnia: *Sound Sleeper** and *Super Sleep**. If you wake during the night, replay the CD, or journal some more. *Insomnia**, a frequency CD, can be played all night.

The Universe is a tonal harmony of many sounds, from vibration at the minutest molecular level to the rotation of the planets and solar systems. Great music has many facets: it nourishes and is always strengthening because it attunes us to powerful waves of life energy. However, the healing energies of music cannot come easily to one who is distracted, resistant, critical, impatient, ungrateful, or poorly prepared. How deeply we feel music depends upon how much of ourselves we are willing to give to music. The more we give ourselves to the music we are experiencing, the more the energy will resonate through us. If the music comes to an open heart and willing mind, it will enter and heal us. I believe the words on a poster I saw several years ago say it best:

THE MIND IS LIKE A PARACHUTE
IT ONLY WORKS WHEN IT IS OPEN!

APPENDIX A

MUSIC RECOMMENDATIONS

PRE-NATAL AND INFANCY - " " denotes a single piece;
underlining denotes an album

Composer	Title	Label
Bach, J.S.	"Air on the G String"	
	Bach for Breakfast	Phillips
Burgland, Erik	Angel Paradise	*
Brahms	"Lullaby"	
Debussy	"Clair de Lune"	
Hart, Mickey	Music to be Born By	
Humperdinck	"Children's Prayer" from Hansel & Gretel	
Massenet	"Meditation" from Thais	
Mascagni	"Intermezzo" from Cavalleria Rusticana	
McDonald-Delos, S.	World of the Harp	
Monroe Institute	Opening the Way - 8 tape album to support Pregnancy & Childbirth	
Mozart	Mozart for Mothers to Be	Phillips
Mozart	Mozart for Meditation	Phillips
Murook, Hajime	Lullaby from the Womb	
Pachelbel	"Canon in D"	
Parents Magazine	Lullaby Album	Angel Records
	Playtime Album	
Saint Saens	"The Swan" from Carnival of Animals	
Schumann	"Traumerei" from Scenes from Childhood	
Tchaikovsky	"Andante Cantabile"	
	"Panorama" from Sleeping Beauty	
Transitions 2	Music to Help Baby Sleep	Placenta
Webber, Julian	Lullaby	
Phillips Wolf-Ferrqui	"Jewels of the Madonna"	

*available at www.InnerHarmonyHealthCenter.com

CHILDREN - All of the above are recommended, plus those listed below.

Composer/Artist	Title	Label
Bach	Bach at Bedtime	Phillips
	Bach at Breakfast	Phillips
	Baroque at Bathtime	Phillips
Beethoven	Beethoven at Bedtime	Phillips
Britten, Benjamin	"Young Persons Guide to the Orchestra"	
Callanan, Tom	Come On and Sing Along	Crackerbarrell
Callanan & Shapiro	Let's Clean Up Your Act	Crackerbarrell
Classical*	Classical Kids Boxed Set includes:	
	Mr. Bach Comes to Call	
	Vivaldi's Ring of Mystery	
	Beethoven Lives Upstairs	
	Mozart's Fantasy	
English, Logan	Woody Guthrie's Children's Songs	Folkways
Glazer, Tom	Lets Sing Fingerplays	CMS
Gutherie, Woody	Songs to Grow On	Folkways
Hinton, Sam	I'll Sing You a Story	Folkways
Jabberwocky	Stories	Crackerbarrell
Jenkins, Ella	Rhythms of Childhood	Scholastic
	My Street Begins at My House	Folkways
	Growing Up with Ella Jenkins	Folkways
	You'll Sing a Song and I'll Sing a Song	Folkways
Kith & Kin	For No Good Reason at All	Crackerbarrell
Mills, Alan	14 Numbers, letters and Animal Songs	Folkways
Morgans	Soundings for the Whale	Crackerbarrell
Muppets	Muppet Musicians of Bremen	Children's Records of America
Paton, Sandy	I've Got a Story	Folk-Legacy
Prokoviev	Peter and the Wolf	
Raven, Nancy	Lullabies & Other Children's Songs	Pacific Cascades
	People and Animal Songs	Pacific Cascades
Rimsky-Korsakov	"Flight of the Bumblebee"	
Ritchie, Jean	Marching Across the Green Grass	Folkways
Rosenshontz*	It's the Truth	RS Records
	Sharo It	"
	Rock 'n Roll	"
Saint Saens	"Carnival of the Animals"	
Seeger, Peggy	Animal Folksongs for children	Folkways
Seeger, Pete	Birds, Beasts, Bugs and Little Fishes	"
	Birds, Beasts, Bugs and Bigger Fishes	"

CHILDREN Continued

Seeger, Pete	<u>American Game and Activity Songs for children</u> "	
	<u>American Folk Songs for Children</u>	Folkways
Shapiro, Ann	<u>Hokey Pokey</u>	Crackerbarrell
Shapiro,Ann	<u>Because I'm Your Mama</u>	Crackerbarrell
Windham Hill for children	Story Tapes:	
	Velveteen Rabbit; Pecos Bill;	
	How the Rhinoceros Got His Skin; etc.	
Winter, Paul	<u>Callings</u>	

TEENS - underlining denotes album title

Composer	Title	Label
	<u>Heavy Classix</u>	
Bach, J.S.	Toccata and Fugue in D Minor	
de Falla	Ritual Fire Dance	
Gershwin	Rhapsody in Blue	
Gorecski	Symphony #3	
Hemi-Sync	<u>Concentration</u>	*
	<u>Remembrance/Concentration</u>	*
	<u>Illumination</u>	*
	<u>Percussion Polynesiennes</u>	Playa Sound
Ravel	Bolero	
Rimsky-Korsakov	Capriccio Espagnol	
	Flight of the Bumblebee	
	Procession of the Nobles	
Respighi	Pines of Rome (last movement)	
Rodrigo	Guitar Concerto de Aranjuez	
Rossini	William Tell Overture	
Tchaikovsky	War of 1812 Overture	
	Capriccio Italian	
Wagner	Ride of the Valkyries	

*available from www.InnerHarmonyHealthCenter.com

COGNITIVE WORK - underlining denotes album title

Composer/Artist	Title	Label
Andre, Maurice	Baroque Trumpet Concerti	
Bach, C.P.E.	Symphony #2	
Bach, J.S. *	Symphony in C Major	
	Lute Suite in E	
	Symphony in D Major	
	Prelude & Allegro in E flat	
	Symphony in G minor	
	Flute Concerto in G minor	
	Choral Prelude in A Major	
	Flute concertos	
	Fantasia in G Major	
	Greatest Hits of 1720	
	Five Concerti after Vivaldi	
	Brandenburg Concertos	
	Canonic Variations & Toccata	
	Parkening Plays Bach	
	The Goldberg Variations (played by Glen Gould)	
Bach, W.	Symphony in D Minor	
Beethoven	Piano Concerto #5 in E flat Major	
	Concerto for Violin in D	
Boccherini	3 Quintets for Guitar & Strings	
Boyce	Symphony Op. #2	
Brahms	Concerto for violin in D Major	
Corelli, A	Concerti Grossi, Op.4: No.4, 10, 11, 12	
	Concerti Grossi, Op.6: No. 3,5,8,9	
Duo Company	Baroque Music for Duo Guitar	
Gregorian Chant		
Handel	Concertos for Organ	
	Music from Royal Fireworks	
	Water Music	
	Concerti Grossi, Op. 6	
	Concerti Grossi, Op.3: 1,2,3,5	
	Concertos for Harp & Orchestra	
	Four Trio Sonatas	
Haydn	Symphony #87 in F Major	
	Violin Concerto #1 in C	
	Symphony #69 in C Major	
	Violin Concerto #1 in G	
	Symphony #63 in C Major	
	Oboe concerto	

Haydn	Symphony #78 in C Minor	
	Symphony #22 in E Flat	
	Symphony #44 in E Minor	
	String Quartet Op.76 in d Minor	
Hemi-Sync(Monroe Inst.)	Concentration	*
	Remembrance	*
	Baroque Garden	*
	Illumination	*
Lind Institute	Classical Harmonies	*
Locatelli	Concerti Grossi, Op. 5: No. 6,7,8	
Marco & Liuia	The Classical Brazilian Guitar	
Mozart	Symphonies #1 to #17	
	Concerto #23 in A Major	
	Violin Concertos (2ND Movements)	
	Quintet for Clarinet in A	
	Concerto for Horn	
	Rhondo for Violin in D	
	Piano concerto #18 in B Flat	
	Sonatas for Flute	
Paganini	Concerto Grossi, Op.5, No. 6,7,8	
	Violin Concerto #4 in F Major	
Relax with the Classics	Classical Harmonies	*
Scarlatti	Symphony #2 for Flute, Trumpet & Strings	
Super Learning CDs		
Teleman	Instrumental Concertos	
Vivaldi	Five Concertos for Flute and Chamber Orchestra	
	Concerto for Lute and Mandolin	
	Six Flute concerti, Op. 10	
	Three Concertos for Viola	
	Two Concertos for Mandolin	

*available from www.InnerHarmonyHealthCenter.com

ENERGY RAISERS - underlining indicates album title.

Composer/Artist	Title	Label
Big Band Music		
Beethoven	Piano Concerto #5	
Bolling	<u>Suite for Flute and Jazz Piano</u> (1st Movement)	
Brahms	Symphony #2 (4th movement)	
<u>Baby Dance</u>		
Copland	Fanfare for the Comman Man	
	Rodeo	
Dukas	LaPeri	
Dvorak	Slavonic Dances	
	Symphony #7 (3rd Movement)	
Elgar	Pomp and Circumstance	
Enesco	Rumanian Rhapsody #1 and #2	
Handel	Halleluia Chorus" from The Messiah	
Holst	Military Suite #1 and #2 for Winds	
Irish Jigs and Reels		
Liszt	Hungarian Rhapsody #1 and 2	
Mozart	<u>Mozart for Morning Coffee</u>	Phillips
Mouret	Fanfares	
Moussorgsky	"Great Gate of Kiev" from Pictures at an Exhibition	
Rimsky-Korsakov	Cappricio Espagnol	
	Procession of the Nobles	
Rossini	William Tell Overture	
Schubert	March Militaire	
Shostakovich	"Polka" from Age of Gold	
Sibelius	"Alla Marcia" from Karelia	
Tchaikovsky	March Slav	
	Capriccio Italian	
Verdi	"Triumphal March" from Aida	
Wagner	Overture to Die Meistersinger	
	"Ride of the Valkyries"	
Winter, Paul	<u>Earthbeat</u>	

GRIEVING

Composer/Artist	Title	Label
Bach	B Minor Mass	
Brahms	Requiem	
Gorescki	Symphony #3	
Grieg	"Ase's Death" from Peer Gynt Suite #1	
Haydn	Cello concerto in D Major (2nd Movement)	
Marcello	Oboe Concero in C Minor (2nd Movement)	
Mozart	Requiem	
Pachelbel	Canon in D	
Schumann, Wm.	"When Jesus Wept" from New England Tryptich	
Sibelius	"Swan of Tuenello"	
Verdi	Requiem	
Villa Lobos	Bachianas Brasileiras #5	

GUIDED IMAGERY - Background music for guided imagery exercises.

Hemi-Sync	Cloudscapes	*
	Inner Journey	*
Oliver, Jim	Music for Relaxation	
Wild, Chuck	Liquid Mind series	Real Music.com

available from www.InnerHarmonyHealthCenter.com

HEALTH RELATED - underlining indicates album title.
*CDs available from www.InnerHarmonyHealthCenter.com

Over All Tune Up

Beaulieu, J.	Calendula	*
	Sonic Chakra Healer frequencies)	*
Ison, David	Balance	
Shapeshiffter	ReJuva	

Addiction

Hemi-Sync	H+ De-Tox	
	DeHab	
	Deep Relaxation	*
	Energy walk	*
	Opening the Heart	*
	Shaman's Heart	*
	So Chord	*
Jonas	Forgiveness	*
	Meeting Your Spirit Guide	*
	Blessings	*

Anger Expression

Heavy Classix		
Bach, J.S.	Toccata & Fugue in D Minor	
Beethoven	Egmont Overture	
Brahms	Piano Concerto #1	
Ginastera	Estancia	
Hemi-Sync	Shaman's Heart	*
Holst	"Mars" from The Planets	
Janacek	Sinfonietta	
Jonas	Forgiveness	*
Orff	"O Fortuna" from Carmina Burana	
Poulenc	Concerto for Organ, Tympanii, & Strings	
Rheinberger	Organ concertos	
Saint Saens	Symphony #3 for Organ (4th movement)	
Tchaikovsky	Symphony #5 (4th Movement)	
Verdi	"Dies Irae" from Requiem	
Wagner	"Ride of the Valkyries"	

Anxiety

Ison, David	Balance	
Jonas, S.	Anxiety Series	*
	Blessings	*
	Deep Relaxation	*
	Color Relax/The Beach	*
Frequency CDs	Digest Aid	*
	PTSD	*
	Stress Buster	*

Anxiety Continued

Lind Institute	Largo	*
	Classical Interlude	*
Hemi-Sync	H+Relax	*
	So Chord	*

Blood Pressure

Hemi-Sync	Deep Journeys	*
	Into the Deep	*
	Inner Journey	*
	So Chord	*
Ison, David	Balance	
Jonas	Blessings	*
	Cardiac Healing	*
	Deep Relaxation	*
Frequency Cds	Oxygenator	*
	Stress Buster	*

Breathing

Frequency CDs	**Breathe Aid**	*
	Oxygenator	*
Jonas	Respiratory Package	*
	Color Relax/The Beach	*
	Deep Relaxation	*
Hemi-Sync	Lung Repairs	*

Cancer

HemiSync	Chemotherapy Companion	*
	Cancer Treatment Pkg	*
	The Visit	*
	Opening the Heart	*
Jonas	Pain Package	*
	Meeting Your Spirit Guide	*
	Forgiveness	*
	Blessings	*
	Deep Relaxation	*
Frequency CDs	DNA/RNA Enhancer	*
	Oxygenator	*

Dental Work - Listener preference is VERY important.

Cater-Garrett	"Keep on the Sunny Side" from Where the Lillies Bloom
Dirgo	Serenade
Dvorak	Slavonic Dance #4 in F Major
Gorden-Warren	"The More I See You" Boston Pops
Handel	"Air" from Water Music
Joplin	"The Sting"
Mahler	Ressurection Symphony (Intermezzo)
McGarrigie	"Walking Song" on Dancer with the Bruised Knee
Mozart	Piano concerto #21 (2nd Movement)
Pachalbel	Canon in D

Depression

Hemi-Sync	The Visit	*
Jonas	Forgiveness	*
	Deep Relaxation	*
	Color Relax/The Beach	*
	Blessings	*
	Meeting Your Spirit Guide	*
Frequency CDs	Bi-Polar Disorder	*

Heart Problems

Strauss, J.	Blue Danube Waltz	
Chopin	Waltzes	
	Golden Age of Viennese Music	
Tango Music		
Jonas, S.	Cardiac Healing	*
	Deep Relaxation	*
	Cardiac Care Series	*
	Forgiveness	*
	Blessings	*
Frequency CDs	Oxygenator	*

Indigestion

Bach	Bach for Breakfast	Phillips
Frequency CD	Digest Aid	*

Insomnia

	Adagio	Decca
	Adagio II	Celestial Harmonies
	Magnum Mysterium	Celestial harmonies
Bach	Bach at Bedtime	Phillips
	Air on the G String	
Brahms	Lullaby	
	Brahms at Bedtime	Phillips
Debussy	Afternoon of a Faun	
Jonas	Insomnia Series	*
	Color Relax/The Beach	*
Massenet	"Meditation" from Thais	
Mozart	Mozart at Midnight	Phillips
Pachelbel	Canon in D	
Palestrina	Pope Marcellus Mass	
Rachmaninov	Vespers	
Schubert	Ave Maria	
Schumann	Traumerei	
Hemi-Sync	Sound Sleeper	*
	Deep Journey	*
	Cloudscapes	*
	Midsummer Night	*
	Into the Deep	*
	Super Sleep	*
	Mystic Realm	
	Sleeping through the Rain	*
	So Chord	*
	Inner Journey	*

Jet Lag

Hemi-Sync	Catnapper	*
	Energy Walk	*
Jonas	Deep Relaxation	*
Frequency CD	Sonic Chakra Healer	*

Meals

Before	Lively music to speed up gastric juices
During	NO brass instruments; quiet music

Paralysis

Brahms	Hungarian Dances
Rossini	William Tell Overture
Sousa	marches
Hemi-Sync	<u>Stroke Recovery Series</u> (6 tape set) *

Respiratory Problems (see Breathing)

Surgery

Lind	<u>Classical Interludes</u>	*
Hemi-Sync	<u>Emergency Treatment Series</u>	*
	<u>So Chord</u>	*
	<u>Sound Sleeper</u>	*
	<u>Super Sleep</u>	*
Frequency CDs	<u>Sonic Chakra Healer</u>	*
	<u>Oxygenator</u>	*

HOSPITAL IN-PATIENT

Jonas, S.	General In-Patient Series	*
Any albums listed under "Anxiety" or "Relaxation"		

IMAGERY PRODUCING MUSIC - * indicates music good for first time listening

Beethoven	Symphony #6 (2nd movement)
Brahms	Symphony #1 (Allegretto)
	Symphony #4 (Andante Moderato)
Britten	Simple Symphony (Sentimental Sarabande)
Copland	Appalacian Spring
Debussy	Nocturnes (Sirens)
	Preludes (Girl with the Flaxen Hair)
	Danses Sacred and Profane
	Afternoon of a Faun
Delius	La Calinda (Koanga)
Dvorak	Legends
Grieg	*Shepherd Boy
	*Peer Gynt Suite (Morning)

IMAGERY PRODUCING MUSIC Continued

Groffe	*Grand Canyon Suite (Morning)
Haydn	Cello Concerto in C major (Adagio)
Holst	Planets (Venus)
Kalinnikov	Symphony #2 (Andante)
Mendelssohn	Scotch Symphony (Andante)
Moussorgsky	Pictures at an Exhibition (Castle)
	Thaiis (Meditation)
Mozart	Clarinet Quintet (Andante)
	Concerto for Flute and Harp
Pachelbel	Canon in D
Pierne	Concertstuck
Ravel	Daphnes and Chloe
	Intro and Allegro
Resphighi	*Pines of Rome (Gioanicola)
	The Birds (The Dove)
	*Fountains of Rome (The Villa Medici
	Fountain at Sunset)
Shapeshifters	ReJuva
Sibelius	Symphony #2 (Allegretto)
Smetena	The Moldau
Vaughn Williams	*Fantasia on Greensleeves
	To a Lark Ascending
	In the Fen Country
	Symphony #5 (Romanza)
	Rosymedre Prelude
Guided Imagery & Music Children's Tape f romAssoc. for Music & Imagery	

INTENSIVE CARE/CORONARY CARE

Hemi-Sync	Deep Relaxation; Energy Walk	*
Jonas, S.	Intensive Care Series	*
	Cardiac Care Series *	*
Frequency CDs	Oxygenator	*
	Chakra Cleanse	*

PAIN CONTROL - see recommendations in Chapter 8

Hemi-Sync	Deep Relaxation; H+Relax	*
Jonas, S.	Pain Control Series	*

MEDITATION

Bealeiu	Calendula	
Campbell, Don	Crystal Meditation	
Dexter & Burns	The Golden Voyage I, II, IV	
Deuter	Silence is the Answer	
Gamelons of Bali		Musical Heritage Soc.
Halpern, Steven	Anti Frantic Alternative Series	
Horn, Paul	Inside the Taj Mahal	
Hemi-Sync*	Cloudscapes	The Visit
	Inner Journey	Gateway Experience Series
	Into the Deep	Deep Journeys
	Mystic Realms	Shamanic Journey
	So Chord	Winds over the World
Iasos	Angelic Music	
Iobst	Seven Metals (singing bowls)	
Laughton	Harps of the Ancient Temple	
La Sierra	Gymnosphere; Song of the Rose"	
Oldfield	Tubular Bells	
	Tintinabulation	
Wild, Chuck	Liquid Mind series	Real Music.com
Wolff & Hemmings	Tibetan Bells	

*available from www.InnerHarmonyHealthCentre.com

PLAYFUL/MOVEMENT/LIVELY

Anderson	Sleigh Ride
	Typewriter Song
	Syncopated Clock
Bizet	L'Arlesienne Suites #1 and #2
Borodin	Polovetsian Dances from Prince Igor
Brahms	Hungarian Dances
Britten	Young Person's Guide to the Orchestra
Chopin	Waltzes
Copland	Rodeo
Debussy	Festivals
deFalla	Ritual Fire Dance
Delibes	Coppelia
Dukas	The Sorcerer's Apprentice
Enesco	Rumanian Rhapsodies #1 and #2
Gliere	Russian Sailor's Dance
Gounod	Funeral March of a Marionette
Grofe'	Grand Canyon Suite

Haydn	Toy Symphony
Irish jigs and reels	
Kabalevsky	The Commedians (Gallop)
Liszt	Grand Gallop Chromatique
Mendelssohn	Symphony #4
	Midsummer's Night Dream
	The Hebrides
Milhaud	Scaramouche (piano duet)
Moussorgsky	Pictures at an Exhibition
	Night on Bald Mountain
Mozart	Overture to The Magic Flute
Offenbach	Gaite Parisienne
Ponchielli	Dance of the Hours
Prokofiev	Peter and the Wolf
	Lt. Kiji Suite
Ravel	Mother Goose Suite
Respighi	Pines of Rome
Rimsky-Korsakov	Scheherzade
	Capriccio Espagnol
Rimsky-Korsakov	Flight of the Bumblebee
	Dance of the Tumblers
Rossini	William Tell Overture
Saint Saens	Carnival of the Animals
Shostakovich	Age of Gold (Polka)
Strauss, J.	Blue Danube Waltz
	Polkas and dances
Strauss, R.	Til Eulenspiegel's Merry Pranks
Stravinsky	Firebird Suite
	Petrouchka
	Rite of Spring
	History of a Soldier
Tchaikovsky	Nutcracker Suite
	Dances from Swan Lake
	Dances from Sleeping Beauty
Wagner	Magic Fire Music from The Valkyries
Weber	Invitation to the Dance
Winter, Paul	Common Ground
	Earthbeat

RELAXATION/STRESS REDUCTION
Classical Selections -

Composer/Artist	Title	Label
	Andante	Celestial Harmonies
	Andante II	Celestial Harmonies
Allen, Nancy	A Celebration for Harp	
Anonymous 4	An English Ladymass	Harmonia Mundi
	The Lily and the Lamb	Harmonia Mundi
Bach, J.S.	Air on the G String	
	Jesu, Joy of Man's Desiring	Morman Tabernacle Choir
	Bach at Bedtime	Phillips
	6 Suites; Sonatas in G & D	Mercury
	Baroque at Bathtime	Phillips
Beethoven	Symphony #6 (2nd movement)	
	Piano Concerto #5 (2nd Movement)	
	Beethoven for Book Lovers	Phillips
Brahms	Waltzes	
	Brahms at Bedtime	Phillips
Bruch	Scottish Fantasy	
Canteloube	Songs of the Auvergne	Erato
	Classics by the Sea	
Chopin	Waltzes	
Debussy	Clair de lune	
	Dances Sacred and Profane (harp)	
	The Sea	
	Engulfed Cathedral	
	Girl with the Flaxen Hair	
	The Petite Suite (En Bateau)	
Field, John	15 Nocturnes for Piano	
Dvorak	Symphony #9 "New World" (2nd Movement)	
Gluck	Orpheus & Euridcye (Minuet)	
Grieg	Peer Gynt Suite #1	
	Holberg Suite	
Grofe'	Grand Canyon Suite (Sunrise)	
Handel	The Messiah	
Holst	The Planets (Venus)	
Humperdinck	Hansel & Gretel (Children's Prayer)	
Kapsberger	Libro Quarto........	Astree
Kreisler	Leibesfreud; Leibesleid	
Mahler	Songs of a Wayfarer (vocal)	
Marcello	Oboe Concerto #21 in C (Andante)	
Marsalis (Performer)	Romances for Saxophone	
Mozart	Piano Concerto #21 in C (Andante)	
	Eine Kleine Nacht Musik	

Classical Stress Reduction Continued

Mozart	Mozart at Midnight	Phillips
	Mozart for Meditation	Phillips
	Mozart for Mothers to Be	Phillips
	Mozart for Morning Coffee	Phillips
	Night Tracks	Teldec
Pachelbel	Canon in D	
Puccini	Madama Butterfly (Humming Chorus)	
Parkening, C. (Perfomer)	Parkening Plays Bach (guitar)	
Rachmaninoff	Symphony #2	
	Piano Concerto #2	
	Vespers	
Ravel	Pavanne for a Dead Princess	
	Clouds	
	Le Tombeau de couperin	
Relax with the Classics	Largo	*
	Classical Interludes	*
Rangell, A. (pianist)	A Recital of Intimate Works	Dorian
Respighi	Fountains of Rome	
	Pines of Rome (Pines of Giancolo)	
	Three Botticelli Pictures	
	The Birds (The Dove)	
	Ancient Airs and Dances	
Satie	Gymnopedie I,II, III	
Vaughn Williams	The Lark Ascending	
	Prelude to Rosymedre	
	Fantasia on Greensleeves	
	In the Fen Country	
Vivaldi	Four Seasons	
	Concerto in D (Adagio)	
	Concerto in B flat (Andante)	
Wagner	Tannhauser (Evening Star)	
Yost, Kelly (Performer)	Piano Reflections	

Non-Classical Albums - Listed by performer and album title

Barenboim	Mi Buenos Aires Querido
Bolling, Claude	Suite for Flute and Jazz Piano
	Suite for Guitar and Piano
Bream, Julian & Williams,John	Julian & John (guitars)
Burton & Corea	Crystal Silence (vibraphone and piano)
Darling & Jones	Amber (cello & piano)
Flower & Brown	Chords & Thyme

Non-Classical Albums Continued

Gordon, David & Steve	Garden of Serenity (nature sounds & music)
	Onenss
Goldman, Jonathan	Frequencies: Sounds of Healing
Halpern	Spectrum Suite (synthesizer)
	Comfort Zone
Iasos	Elixer (synthesizer)
Ison, David	Spring; Summer; Fall; Winter
	Therasound.com
Jazz for Quiet Times	32jazz
Jones, Michael	Seascapes (piano)
	Pianoscapes (piano)
Kelly, Georgia	Seaspace (harp)
	A Journey Home (harp & Cello)
Kobialka	Path of Joy (synthesizer)
	Pachelbel Canon
Lee	Celestial Spaces for Koto
Miller, Emmett	The Healing Journey (guided relaxation)
	Northern Lights
Oldman, Coyote	Tear of the Moon
Oliver, Jim	Music for Relaxation
Rampal & Laskin	Japanese Melodies for Flute & Harp
Renbourn	The Lady and the Unicorn
	Sir John Alot of
Robertson, Kim	Gratitude (harp and cello)
Seerie	And the Stars Go With You
Spheris	Desires of the Heart
Stoltzman, R.	Begin Sweet World (clarinet)
	Spirits
Trio Roccoco	Norwegian Wood
Webber, J.	Lullaby Phillips
Wild, C.	Liquid Mind series Real Music
Williams, J	Echoes of London (guitar)
Winston, G.	Autumn (piano)
Zamfir	Romantic Flute of Pan (panpipes)
Hemi-Sync*	Deep Relaxation Midsummer Night
	Into the Deep Inner Journey
	Cloudscapes Energy Walk
	Winds over the World Mystic Realms
	Deep Relaxation Color Relax

available at: www.InnerHarmonyHealthCenter.com

154

SOUL MUSIC - Listed by composer and composition; underline denotes album title.

	Ave Maria -St. John's College Choir	
Ancient Echoes	"Rejoice Now Heavenly Powers"	BMG Classics
Andrews, Joel	Gloria for Gaia	harpofgold.com
Bach, J.S.	Come Sweet Death	
	Little Fugue in G	
	Mass in B Minor (Sanctus)	
Barber	Adagio for Strings	
Beethoven	Symphony #1 (Adagio)	
	Missa Solemnis	
	Piano Concerto #5 (2nd Movement)	
	Symphony #6 (2nd Movement)	
	Symphony #9 [Finale]	
Brahms	Piano Concerto #2 (Andante)	
	Violin Concerto (2nd Movement)	
	German Requiem	
Bruckner	Symphony #8 (3rd Movement)	
Cantelube	Songs of the Auvergne (Pastourelle)	Erato
	Days of Majesty	MusicfromGod.com
Debussy	Reverie	
Dvorak	Symphony #9 (Largo)	
Elgar	Enigma Variations (Variations 8 and 9)	
Enya	Watermark	
Faure	"In Paradisum" Reguiem	
Goldman, Jonathan	Holy Harmony	
Gregorian Chant	Messes Gaudete & Laetare Abby of St. Pierre of Solesme	
Gounod	St. Cecilia's Mass (Sanctus)	
Handel	The Messiah: *And he shall feed his flock;*	
	Halleluha Chorus	
	Xerxes (Largo)	
Holst	The Planets [Neptune]	
Hykes	Harmonic Meetings	
Humperdinck	Hansel & Gretel (Children's Prayer)	
Mahler	Symphony #5 (2nd Movement)	
Magnum Mysterium		Celestial Harmonies
Mozart	Versperae Solemnas: "Sanctus"	
	Requiem	
Pachelbel	Canon in D	
Pallestrina	Pope Marcellus Mass	
The Power and the Majesty	Robert Shaw Chorale	Telarc
Rachmaninoff	Vespers	
Ravel	Piano Concerto #5 (2nd Movement)	
Resphighi	Pines of Rome (Pines of Giancola)	
Rodrigo	Guitar Concerto (2nd Movement)	

SOUL MUSIC Continued

Rutter, John	Requiem	
Sanctus - Meditations for the Soul		Archiv
Schumann, Wm.	New England Triptych: "When Jesus Wept"	
Shantala	Love Window : "Amba Parameshwari"	
		shantalamusic.com
Shostakovich	Piano Concerto #5 (2nd Movement)	
Sibelius	Swan of Tuonela	
	Symphony #5	
Spirituals in Concert	Kathleen Battle and Jesse Norman	DG
Strauss, R.	Death & Transfiguration	
	"Breit Uber Mein Haupt" (Sung by Beverly Sills)	
Vaughn Williams	Fantasia on a Theme of Thomas Tallis	
	5 Mystical Songs	
	Concerto for Oboe (2nd Movement)	
	To a Lark Ascending	
von Bingen, Hildegard	Feather on the Breath of God	
Wagner	Prelude to Act 1 of Lohengrin	
Walton, Wm.	Henry V (Touch Her Soft Lips)	
Wild, Chuck	Liquid Mind IV	Real Music
Winter, Paul	Missa Gaia	

APPENDIX B

EQUIPMENT RECOMMENDATIONS

Vibrating Mats, Beds, Chairs

www.somatron.com
www.klini.com
www.sosoundsolutions.com
www.vibroacoustic.org

Transducer Speakers

www. biowaves.com
www.vibroacoustic.org

Pillow Speakers

www.InnerHarmonyHealthCenter.com

Ecophone(bone conduction listening device)   www.ecophone.com

APPENDIX C

MUSIC RESOURCES

BOOKS

Aldridge, David. Music Therapy Research and Practice in Medicine. Athenaeum Press, Gateshead, Tyne &Wear, London. 1996

Atwater, F. Holmes. "The Hemi-Sync Process." Unpublished Research. The Monroe Institute, Faber, VA. 1997.

Bonny, Helen & Savory, Louis. Music and Your Mind. ICM Press, Port Townsend, WA. 1973.

Campbell, Don.   Introduction to the Musical Brain
      Music: Physician for Times to Come
      The Mozart Effect. Avon Books, N.Y., N.Y. 1997
      Music and Miracles. Quest Books, Wheaton, IL 1992.

Clair, A. A. (1996). Therapeutic Uses of Music With Older Adults. Baltimore, MD: Health Professions Press.

Clines, Manfred. Music, Mind and Brain. Plenum, 1982.

Cousto, Hans. The Cosmic Octave. LifeRhythm, 1988.

Crowley, Brian. Words of Power.

Emoto, M. Messages from Water.

Furman, Charles. Ed. Effectiveness of Music Therapy Procedures. 2nd Edition. NAMT Press, Silver Spring, MD. 1996

Gerber, Richard. Vibrational Medicine. Bear & Co., Santa Fe, NM. 1996. Newer edition available.

Goldman, Jonathan. The Healing Sounds: the Power of Harmonics. Element, 1996.

Hamel, Peter Michael. Through Music to the Self. Shambhala: Boulder, CO. 1976

Hodges, Donald A., Ed. Handbook of Music Psychology. 2nd Edition. IMR Press, University of Texas, San Antonio, TX. 1996.

Horowitz and Puleo. Healing Codes for a Biological Apocolypse. Tetra Hedron Publishing, Idaho. 2001.

Jenny, Hans. Cymatics Vol. I&II. Basilus, 1974.

Kayser, Hans. Akroasis, the Theory of World Harmonics. (Plowshare), 1970.

LaForest, Sandra & MacIovr, Virginia. Vibrations: Healing through Color, Homeopthy and Radionics. N.Y. Samuel Weiser, 1979.

Leland, Kurt. Music and the Soul. Hampton Roads, Charlottesville, VA. 2005.

Loewy, J.. Music therapy pediatric pain management: Assessing and attending to the sounds of hurt, fear, and anxiety. In J. Loewy (Ed.), Music Therapy and Pediatric Pain, (pp. 45-56). Jeffrey Books. 1997

Madaule, Paul. When Listening Comes Alive. Moulin Pub. Norval, Ont. 1993.

Maman, Fabien. The Role of Music in the 21st Century. Tama-Do Press, 1997.

Manners, Peter Guy. Cymatic Therapy. Bretforton, 1976.

Maranto, Cheryl D., Ed. Applications of Music in Medicine. NAMT Press, Silver Spring, MD. 1991.

McClellan, Randall. The Healing Forces of Music. Rockport, MA Element, Inc. 1991.

Menuhin, Yehudi and Davis, Curtis. The Music of Man. Methuen, Inc., N.Y. 1979.

Radha, Swami sivinanda. Mantras: Words of Power. Timeless, 1980.

Rider, Mark. The Rhythmic Language of Health and Disease. MMB Music, Inc., Saint Louis,MO. 1997.

Schneck, D.J. & Berger, Dorita. The Music Effect. Athenaeum Press, Gateshead, New Britain. 2006.

Spintge, Ralph and Droh, Roland, Eds. MusicMedicine. MMB Music, Inc., Saint Louis, MO.1992.

Tame, David. The Secret Power of Music. N.Y.: Destiny Books. 1984.

Taylor, Dale B. Biomedical Foundations of Music Therapy. MMB Music, Inc., Saint Louis, MO.1997.

Wigram, Tony; Saperston, Bruce and West, Robert, Eds. The Art & Science of

Music Therapy: A Handbook. Harwood Academic Publishers, The Netherlands. 1995.

Wigram, T and Dileo, C. Eds. Music Vibration. Jeffery Books, Cherry Hill, NJ. 1997

WEBSITES

Acoustic Brain Research   www.tomkenyon.com

American Music Therapy Assn.   www.musictherapy.org

Assn. of Sound Therapy & Harmonic Studies
       www.arrakis.es/~shamael/english.htm

Aura sounds: Dr. Valerie Hunt's work   www.bioenergyfields.org
     Store for Dr. Hunt's books,tapes,etc.   www.malibupublishing.com

Bach Flower Music   www.bachflowermusic.com

Bible Tones Info   www.reife.com/bible_codes.html
Bible Tones to order   www.healthyworlddistributing.com
Bible Psalms music   www.MusicfromGod.com
Bible Tones Therapy   www.SomaEnergetics.com

BioAcoustics; Sharry Edwards' work   www.soundhealthinc.com

BioAcoustics instruments   www.biowaves.com

Biomedical research in music   www.colostate.edu/depts/cbrm

Chakra & music correlates   www.musicandthesoul.blogspot.com

Challot, Jacotte healing CDs   www.multidimensionalmusic.com

Chant **CDs;**
     Jonathan Goldman's work   www.healingsounds.com
      overtone chanting; David Hykes   www.harmonicworld.com
      ancient chants Mitchell Gibson, M.D;   www.tybro.com

Chronomedicine   www.digipharm.com

Cymatics: Dr. Hans Jenny's work   www.cymaticsource.com

Cymatherapy: Dr. Peter Guy Manners' work   www.cymatherapy.com

DNA music   Susan Alexjander *Sequencia* CD   www.oursounduniverse.com
Elements Sounds: Robert Lloy's work   www.rlloy@jetlink.net

Emoto, Masaru...Messages from Water
                                          www.masaruemoto.net/english/entop.html

Five Elements CD   www.toolsforwellness.com

Heartsongs CD   http://reyfab.bidmc.harvard.edu/heartsongs

Hemi-Sync **CDs**   www.innerharmonyhealthcenter.com

Lambdoma/Pathagorean sound healing   www.lambdoma.com

Maman, Fabien   www.tama-do.com

Medical Resonance Music Therapy from Holland
                                          www.ScientificMusicTherapy.com

Mira coils, clustered H2O, other   www.sound-energy.com

Mozart programmed CDs   www.mozarteffect.com

The Monroe Institute; Bob Monroe's work   www.monroeinstitute.org

Music Therapy Research data base   http://iucairss.utsa.edu
        www.internethealthlibrary.com/therapies/musictherapy-research.html
        www.uwec.edu/rasarla/research

Musicure from Denmark (environmental music)   www.musicure.com

Center for Music Research   www.music.fsu.edu/cmrbro.html

Musical Medicine **CDs;** Dr. Suzanne Jonas' center
                                          www.innerharmonyhealthcenter.com

Music or sound tables/chairs   www.somatron.com
                                              www.neuroacoustic.com
                                            www.sosoundsolutions.com
                                                    www.klini.com
                                              www.vibroacoustic.org

Music Therapy books   www.mmbmusic.com

Prosperity, Creativity, Sensuality, etc., tone **CDs**   www.omagroup.net

Physics of sound research: Dale Pond;   www.supvril.com

Super Learning   www.superlearning.com

Tom Keeley's sound research   www.supvril.com

Dr.Jeffery Thompson   www.neuroacoustic.com

TuningForks ;Bija meditations;
  Dr. John Bealieau;   www.biosonics.com
  Acutonics- Donna Carey's work   www.acutonics.com
  Tama-do - Fabien Maman's work   www.tama-do.com
  Sacred Waves   www.SacredWaves.com

Dr. Alfred Tomatis' work   www.tomatis.com
     www.appliedmusic.com

Vibroacoustic research   www.somatron.com
     www.vibroacoustic.org

APPENDIX D
MUSIC THERAPY CHECK LIST

Date_____ Time_____ am/pm   Name of Practitioner_____

Patient Name_____ Age____ Sex____ Dx:_____

Current Status of Patient(including any recent medications)_____

MUSIC THERAPY GOAL

____Anxiety Decrease   ____Energy Increase   ____Mood:Set

____Bladder Control   ____Exercise Enhancer   ____Meditation

____Boredom Relief   ____Insomnia Decrease   ____Pain

____Breathing Regulation   ____Relaxation

____Heartrate: Stabilize ____BP: Lower   ____BP: Raise

____Lightheadedness   ____Mood: Change to_____

____Concentration Increase   ____Other_____

CONSIDERATIONS

Patient Stats: Equipment Stats:

                                            Condition_____

Cultural Background_____   Batteries_____

Preference for Classical_____ Popular_____ Headphones_____

Current Level of Pain(1-10, 10 is highest)_____

Current Level of Anxiety : High Med   Low

Staff Stats: ____Other staff informed

                  ____Phone ringer turned off

                  ____Sign on door (no interruptions)

CD CHOSEN_____

WHY_____

POST LISTENING EVALUATION

Was the goal successfully achieved? 1(definitely)   2   3(somewhat)   4   5(no)

Patient Comments:

A BRIEF HISTORY OF WESTERN MUSIC

I love music passionately.......... Claude Debussy

In looking at the lists of music recommendations that have been used by professionals for various purposes there is a seemingly narrow body of specific classical music styles for each purpose. For instance, Baroque music is mainly used for cognitive work: music from the late Romantic, Impressionists, and Neo-Romantic is used for imagery; and modern classical music is rarely used at all. This is no accident. The music written during any given period reflects both the society in which the composer lives and the composer (this also applies to the visual arts). An easy example is a Jackson Pollack painting with its drips and dribbles covering the canvas, showing very little obvious organization or meaning. This artist of the 1960's certainly captured the feeling of our Western society which is scattered in interests and searching for meaning and organization; this artist ended his own life. Now listen to classical music by John Cage, a contemporary of Pollack's, and the same feeling will be aroused in most people: discomfort and a desire to stop the music. This is due to the seeming disorganization, disharmony, scattered sounds and energies in the music.

It is therefore helpful to know the characteristics surrounding various time periods in Western music so that one has some general idea of which type of music might be appropriate for a specific purpose. The following brief history of Western music is intended to give the reader a general picture of certain time periods. It is not to be an in depth social commentary or treatise on musical styles. If there are periods that peak your interest more information can be gleaned from the resource books listed in the back of the book.

MUSIC IN THE ANCIENT WORLD

There are no peoples on this planet who did not develop a musical art. It was always a part of any ritual be it religious, spiritual, or associated with war, the hunt, or love. Historians believe that the first musicality was an imitation of nature sounds: birds and other animals, and rhythmic poundings. Surviving instruments from ancient civilizations include a neolithic bone flute from the tombs of Egypt (@ 28,000 B.C.), Chinese stone drums and earthenware pipes (1500 B.C.) and bronze trumpets from the beat bogs of Denmark. Pictures of instruments have survived on cave walls, vases, and building murals, and the literature of Ancient Egypt, Greece, the Bible, and mythology all include descriptions of the importance of music.

In general, ancient discussions of music were either focused on its mathematical properties or its effects on the human system. The Royal Academy at Thebes, Egypt founded in @1580 BC was a place for these discussions. Later, the Greek scientist Pythagoras (582-500 BC) defined the pitch system so music could be replayed with some semblance of accuracy. Before that time each instrument had its own notes uncoordinated with same instruments or different instruments, i.e. if we both had flutes we could not play together because our tones would be dissimilar. The Ancient Greeks gave music a place of honor - it was considered as important as science and philosophy, and became an important medical treatment. It was Pythagoras who taught students how certain musical chords and melodies produced different responses on the body and demonstrated how the right sequence of sounds played musically on an instrument could cure bodily pains, soothe the bereaved, calm anger, and still desire. Roman physicians and priests, too, used music therapy until the Roman empire was completely Christianized. We know very little about these healing melodies as there was no formal system of notation at that time. Even the sound of the instruments can only be conjectured.

The first great era of modern Western music did not occur until after the Dark Ages, after the many wandering, warring tribes settled and became towns, @700-1400AD, commonly termed the Middle or Medieval Period. The music was directly inherited from Sumeria, Egypt, and Greece whose tonal system survived the fall of the Greek and Roman Empires

MEDIEVAL PERIOD - 700-1400AD

Early Medieval - Popular music during this time was made up of songs and lays which preserved legends and folk wisdom. The poet and composer were the same and very often she was also the performer as well. These minstrels were employed by lords or wandered the countryside passing along their songs and learning other songs by rote. Dances and popular tunes were also favored to provide recreation and express the everyday occurrences one experienced on the land and in the family.

Sacred music was centered in the monasteries, which were a market place for the interchange of ideas. Here the monks passed along religious music both by rote memory and a simple system of written symbols. Their music was a single sung line termed "Plain chant" which comprised the mass. The text was based on the religious theology of the time that man is a creature of God's creation, a reflection of him. Therefore, man was seen as in harmony with the angels and the beasts and while listening to music would vibrate harmoniously with himself. The science of music could illuminate through analogy and the cosmic harmonies, and reveal truths about God, the world, and man. It was said at the time that without music no scientific discipline could be perfect. How far afield we are today from these philosophies.

The music of this period, then, was simple and rhythmic and a direct reflection of man's daily activities and feelings of harmony with God.

Gothic Period/Latter Medieval - 1100-1300AD - This was a time of hope, experiment, and religious fervor. The society was dominated by the Crusades and a feudal economy: power was equally shared by the church and the nobility.

Popular song continued to be the transmitter of local and worldly news. It was the time of courtly love, which became the focus of many secular songs. Sacred music remained in the church, ie. not sung out of the monasteries or churches, and only sung by monks, nuns, and clergy. The church mandated that all music be sung: no instruments were to be played in the church as the human voice was the most perfect instrument.

By the 10th Century another voice had been added to the single line of plain chant which paralleled the melody in 4th and 5ths - it was termed "organum". By the 11th Century a low sustained note was under the organum and in the 12th Century a distinct 3rd voice was added, usually sustained notes. The Medievalists were not in a hurry to experiment with music! Every new form was treated as a welcome addition to the older styles, which died slowly or not at all as in the case of the simple minstrel songs. The ideal of sound at this time was one of contrast, both simultaneous and successive. Contrasts were created between male and female voices, between loud and soft, between different instruments, between percussion and instruments, between instruments and voices. The harmonic structure of the music remained very simple, as dictated by the church, so no contrast in harmony or "key" within the musical composition was heard.

By the 13th Century the English had made their contribution to the realm of music with the "invention" of part songs or rounds, cajoles to celebrate holidays and great occasions, and a volume of Crusade songs. These were carried across the channel to the mainland by the wandering minstrels who continued to be an important part of town and court life. Within the courts not only were songs important but dance music, which was played on a variety of instruments.

COMPOSERS during this time were: Ventadorn, Leonin, Perotin, and Hildegarde von Bingen.

Ars Nova - 1300-1450 - The 14th Century was one of great transition, from feudal economy to the beginning of merchant economies, to stronger city states, and to power in the hands of the wealthy who were not necessarily the nobility. This new merchant power along with the nobility, challenged the dominance of the church. The Holy Roman Church found itself with reduced dominance in matters of music and because of a divided papacy, a decline of church authority in all temporal matter. This became a time of political and moral upheaval, an age of fear and disintegration exemplified in several plagues of Black Death and the 100 years wars between France and England (1353-1453). It is difficult to imagine being at war for 3 generations!

During this time the true composer developed in Italy. This was a person who did not necessarily perform, but wrote dance music or madrigals (3 part songs) for others.

In France the Avignon Papal Court became an international school of music composition for the Ars Nova. The composers, called Mannerists, wrote for the courts of a dying feudal nobility, ignoring the new forms looming in Italy. They focused on secular songs: ballads, virelai, and rondeaus, becoming virtuoso in their method of notation.

England continued to popularize cajoles and sacred polyphony (several independent musical lines sung together) and brought the motet form to its height (motet is a sacred 3 part song that had a solo top voice).

The 15th Century continued the transition from church to secular power and feudal to merchant economy. By the end of the century a new type of citizen had arisen and firmly taken a place in the world: the middle class person. This class had not only a dwelling like the poor, but also had a living room separate from the kitchen and sleeping rooms. She also had time to study and money to hire tutors. Leonardo de Vinci was a perfect embodiment of this new man.

Music now incorporated a definite 4th part, the addition being a low contra tenor (or bass). These four parts were now used to create a unified and harmonious vocal price, a vertical movement, as opposed to the previous part music whose lines moved independently of one another. The harmonic structure continued to remain simple.

COMPOSERS during this time were: Machaunt, Landini, Ockeghem, Dufay, Isacc, and DesPrez.

RENAISSANCE - late 15th C. to last 3rd of 16th C.

The Renaissance was the culmination of the preceding two centuries of transition. Everything in this new world was different including the way man saw himself. Not satisfied any longer with being just a creation of God, he now saw himself as the NOBLEST creation of God AND A CREATOR in his own right! Everything now centered on the interests of man, not his centering on God. He began to explore himself and the world. The greatest achievements were in the visual arts and architecture which could portray, honor, and commemorate man. These achievements were sponsored y persons of enormous wealth for their own aggrandizement. At this same time came the invention of the printing press, which would change the world forever. Now all persons had the opportunity to learn to read and gain knowledge for themselves.

Within the weakened church splits continued to occur. The largest split occurred with the assistance of Martin Luther and would have enormous impact on liturgical music. Music in the new Protestant sect could now be performed by other than clergy or religious personnel, and most importantly, the congregation was now allowed to sing. New music flourished, particularly in private chapels, which were a symbol of status and power. Songs (hymns) for the congregation became an important compositional medium for German composers by the end of the Renaissance. Singing of spiritual songs for private worship was encouraged and each country developed its own liturgical music. The Holy Roman Church mass expanded into a significant and autonomous work that included secular songs among the melodies. The overall effect of the music was of voices moving together, both vocal music and instrumental music.

Not only was man exploring the geographical world at this time but also philosophy, science, architecture, and the arts. Musical compositions expanded in areas previously regulated by the church: namely pitch and chromatics. Rhythms were also now used significantly to create overall shapes, i.e., different rhythms for different sections, but keeping an overall repeated rhythmic pattern to effect a sense of cohesion.

The English motet expanded into four parts having very little embellishment. Song style also expanded into four parts with each country developing their own form. Folk songs continued to travel from country to country. The folk ballade, sung by street performers known as buskers, became the gossip column of the people. The English printed these folk songs and hawked them on the streets.

As we can see, up until the end of the 16th Century music composed had four primary focuses: 1) Religious: for the worship of God; 2) for the passing on of news; 3) for light entertainment in the courts: dances, love and hunt songs; and 4) as a release from day to day living of hard work and/or war.

By the end of the Renaissance each country was developing its own form of Protestantism with ensuing liturgical styles and music. At the same time, the emphasis in music shifted from private chapels to private salons. Here musicians specialized in performing either sacred or secular music. Some of the most popular forms were:

Madrigal - for 3-8 voices, usually 5
> the theme of most songs being the lover who was rejected or bereaved (somewhat like our Country & Western music!).

Glee - men's part song - this was the beginning of the Glee Club.

Catches - unison rounds containing puns which were often very course and funny, so course that these were only seen fit to be sung by men.

Barbershop - the typical barbershop of the Renaissance always had a banjo-like cittern on hand for customers to play and sing while waiting to be shaved and trimmed. It soon became a place to sing and harmonize whether one needed the services of the barber or not. Can you image people today singing while waiting in lines?!...

In reaction to he extremes of polyphony (some masses and motets contained 20-40 parts!) the single simple one line melody became very popular. The solo madrigal called "lute song or air", had a fine poem as text, professional singer/lutenist to perform it, and an accompanist on viola da gamba (early cello) who provided a reinforcing bass line. At this time the precursor of the modern opera was forming: the Drama per Musica. Based on mythological, allegorical, or classical stories, a monody was sung free style (termed "recitative") and alternated with a chorus, dances, and instrumental interludes.

Instrumental music paralleled vocal music in its inclusion of four distinct musical lines. These were played by balanced sets of instruments called "a chest". A chest of strings would include the fore runner of our modern string quartet, a chest of recorders would have 4 different sized recorders imitating the four vocal ranges: soprano, alto, tenor, bass. After exhausting the number of chests one could invent, the end of the 16th C. was devoted to mixing chests into consorts so a variety of instruments were now found playing together. The Italians formed a larger consort that was the beginning of our modern orchestra, and composed a specific form for them: the concerto grosso. This was the first musical form specifically written for a large group of specific instruments for pure listening. Most instrumental music up until this time was for dancing or as an interlude between songs.

Dance music was still the most popular instrumental music. Most often the music was compiled into dance suites that contained several pairs of dances. These pairs were contrasts in rhythm and tempo and allowed for an interesting variety of steps.

Instruments to accompany singers included the organ and lute, which was the most popular instrument of the Renaissance. There were instructional books written, the first for any instrument, collections of published music, competitions, and lute tutors. And a new phenomena occurred: a perceptive, receptive audience, who came together to listen and appreciate a performance. The stage was now set for the creation of a new dimension in music: professional composers, professional musicians, and formal concerts.

COMPOSERS of this period were: Dunstable, Sassos, Palestrina, Morley, Gabrielli, Monteverdi, and Gesualdo.

BAROQUE - 1600-1750

This century and a half was dominated by the growth of an absolute monarchy, colonization in the world, ornament and opulence, all of which were directly reflected in art, architecture, fashion and music. All of these came together into grand theater - OPERA - where no expense was spared. It was a spectacle where all the new inventions of the arts were incorporated to produce grand illusion (flying, clouds, weather, etc.). Italy became the progenitor and supporter of this grand art. The soloist became a specialist in vocal techniques and was revered by the audience. The ideal voice emulated by all others was the high voice of prepubescent boys. To keep this vocal quality, boys with beautiful voices were castrated before puberty to prevent the voice from dropping; these singers became known as castrati.

To imitate this high, clear vocal quality on an instrument, the violin was perfected through the hands of such masters as Stradevari and Guanari. The new ideal of musical fabric became the violin and/or voice with viola d gamba (early cello playing the bass line) with harpsichord accompaniment. The later was played by a competent musician but inconspicuous in the performance. An orchestra could also accompany a solo instrument, the new Italian form being termed the "concerto". It was a large work in three movements most obviously different in their tempos: Moderate, Slow, Fast.

Other larger musical forms evolved during this time:

Cantata:	solo voice with basso continuo
Oratorio	small opera form based on a Biblical text and performed without the theatrics of opera
Sonata	a concerto for solo instrument accompanied by basso continuo and harpsichord
Concerto Grosso:	this form expanded further into a small instrumental solo group alternating with the larger group

In France, Louis XIV brought the arts to new heights and importance (at the expense of the common man). It was a time of musical splendor with the importing of Italian opera, outdoor spectacles including carousels, and ballets. The latter was the French contribution to the arts. They felt it was the perfect art form: a combination of instrumental color with dance and artistic sets. It was this love of instrumental color that led them to invent a variety of different sounding instruments. They also became the leader in modern keyboard style on harpsichord and clavichord. Non Versailles culture centered in the salons of the wealthy and influential. Interestingly, it was the wives who were known for their salon entertainments that included the sharing of music, poetry, plays, and discussions of science and politics. The lute and guitar solo work, keyboard, and popular songs filled the evening's musical program.

After the death of Elizabeth I in the early 1600's, English cultural development and interest waned in the hands of the reigning religious groups: Cromwellians and Puritans. These groups were against music and drama and barred their entrance into the country and, as much as possible, into private homes. This dearth of culture was followed on the heels by both an outbreak of the Black Plague and the London fire in the 1660's. Charles I restoration to the throne at about this time brought French and Italian musical forms into England fostering the growth of their own compositional form: the oratorio, perfected by Handel.

As Germany was the center of the split in the Catholic Church, the Protestant Church there gained more importance than the royal court so that church music became a specialty of that country. In particular, the German Lutheran church rose as the leader in new musicals with the prolific and inspiring music of J.S. Bach. Weekly he would compose new hymns, cantatas (music for church choruses), preludes and postludes, all for the most grand of instruments - the pipe organ. The royal courts and smaller courts would copy and import music, opera, ballet, etc. from Italy and France.

The society as a whole functioned around the court that governed the way one acted, ate, dressed, played, and interacted. Every act was well thought out before commencing so as not to disobey the rules of etiquette. Clothing was also as stiff, impractical, and confining as the rules of etiquette. On the other hand, clothing, interiors, and architecture were highly decorative. Instrumental music reflected this ornamentation, magnificence, grandeur, and orderliness by the addition of trills and other ornamentations on a note. New developments included additional musical instruments, the perfection of the violin, harpsichord and clavichord. The new forms included cantatas, concerto grosso, overture (prelude to opera or ballet), fugue (complex round for organ or orchestra), and aria (operatic solo). In general, the orchestral music of the Baroque reflected the orderliness of the time: it was rationally conceived, ordered, with little variation in tempo or dynamics within a piece. It did contain contrasts with major and minor tonalities, new harmonies, and contrapuntal styles. It was generally written with a strong melody line supported by the orchestra.

COMPOSERS of this period were:

England - Byrd, Dowland, Purcell, Handel
France   - Lully, Couperin, Rameau
Germany - Schutz, Buxtehude, Pachelbel, J.S. Bach, Teleman
Italy   - Monteverdi, Frescobaldi, Corelli, Scarlatti, Vivaldi

CLASSICAL PERIOD - 1750-1820

With the growth of the middle class and the influence of the salons, Paris became an intellectual hub of the Western world. This essence was greatly reflected in the music. The music was objective, emotionally restrained, had a clear form, and adhered to structural principals. The forms and structures most popular during this time were:

Sonata for solo instrument - 3 movements of Moderate, Slow, Fast

Symphony - for orchestra in 4 movements: Moderate, Slow, Moderate, Dance, and Fast

Popular solo instruments were the harpsichord and clavichord and the newest instrument, the square piano. By the 1780's the piano, with its inexpensive price tag and ability to stay in tune better than the harpsichord or clavichord, was a universal instrument.

The writing of instrumental music was now definitely a skill few persons had (or still have, in my opinion!). Every court sought a resident composer to bring it fame; few succeeded. One such notable at this time was Mozart, the darling of the Austrian courts during the 1780's. It was he who defined the modern classical concerto - a large piece in three movements (Moderate, Slow, Fast) for solo instrument with orchestral accompaniment. Popular solo instruments were the piano and flute. He was prolific, to say the least, leaving an enormous repertoire of symphonies, operas, concertos, and a Requiem before he died at the age of 32. The 1770's were dominated by the great English composer, Haydn, who was then considered the greatest living composer. He was also prolific with respect to concertos, symphonies, sonatas, and oratorios.

New developments within the compositions included the use of :

crescendo - a gradual increase in volume by the entire orchestra
harmonic and rhythmic contrasts within a movement
slurred notes
textural variety - combinations of different instruments in the
     orchestra

The construction of instruments became standardized at this time so orchestras would sound similar and music written for specific instruments could be performed anywhere.

Outside of the concert hall, whether in a court or city, the most popular music continued to be songs and dances, in particular, the waltz. Mozart wrote several for this new dance form which was of a 3/4 meter and stately performed, not at all similar to the waltz form of Old Vienna in the 1880's.

Transition - 1790-1820 - During this 30 year period several major political changes were occurring: the French revolution dethroned the monarchy and replaced it with Napoleon Bonaparte, and the new United States was fighting again in the War of 1812. Clothing styles changed radically from stiff, ornate costumes to Classical flowing styles that reflected these changes. With the change in Paris, Vienna now became the busiest center of musical amusement. Here one could attend opera, dance hall, and the song spiel. Vienna also was home to the most important composer during this time, Ludwig von Beethoven. Although he continued the classical style and structures, and finalized the symphonic form as we know it today, it was the introduction of a new element into music - emotionality - that was his greatest gift. In his music we now identify joy, anger, love, and passion. He also created a different piano style of legato: in a connected manner. With these two new elements, emotionality and legato style, he ushered in the next major period.

COMPOSERS of this period were:
France   - Gretry
Germany - Haydn, J.C.Bach, Gluck, Ditters von Ditters-dorf,
       Mozart, Salieri, Beethoven
Italy   - Puccini, Boccherini, Clementi, Cherubini, Rossini

ROMANTIC PERIOD - 1820-1900

This period is characterized as the century of inventions that created an entirely new world based on industry. The idea of progress was given impetus through the English scientist Charles Darwin and the idea of evolution. It was also a time of redefining man, which was done through a youth movement and became the Age of the Individual. (not unlike our 1960's). The chief spokesperson for this movement was the poet - young, and overpowered by both genius and emotion. All art forms would now be injected with the personal life of the artist and emotion would be its focus.

Music was at the center of Parisian thought and musical life centered on the piano. Frederic Chopin was the darling of Paris salons in the 1830's and 40's and Hungarian Franz Lizst , friend of Chopin's, was the greatest piano virtuoso. Paris also loved Italian opera, the new Romantic ballets, comic opera, and symphonies, particularly those by Berlioz. The cities of Germany represented a triumph of the Romantic view at its most extreme. Robert Schumann embodied this ideal. Described as melancholy in his youth, he swung from extremes, even suicide and despair, to an equally extreme of joy. (He would probably be diagnosed as manic-depressive today). Listening to his music these moods are clearly heard. Vienna was the center of popular music with the dance hall being the most popular. The Strauss family produced beautiful waltzes for these halls, furthering the development of the waltz to its current form.

The pattern of life was changing as the general standard of living in Western Europe rose, along with the level of education. The concept of the audience was also evolving in the concert hall and opera house as well as the outdoor garden and park where bands were popular. In this Age of the Individual, the composer and performer vied for the top place of honor. The former all agreed on melody, harmony, and rhythm as the basic elements of music and added their own personal/emotional influence. The performers adhered strictly to the scores and favored pieces with a slower tempo or with virtuoso passages to show off their abilities. This new virtuoso soloist was now given more opportunity by the composer for improvisation, an area heretofore relegated to the opera singer. Concertos now contained a cadenza where the orchestra or other accompaniment ceases and the soloist is left to improvise on the themes presented in the composition.

Within a few years of Beethoven's death Western music began to break with the ordered conventions of the Baroque and Classical styles.   Brahms labored 20 years to complete his first symphony having thought of Beethoven's symphonies as complete perfection. Several new forms appeared during this time: the Polish mazurka for piano introduced by Chopin, short pieces for piano, program pieces like Chopin ballades and Schumann's "Carnival" (a grouping of short piece).   There were expanded harmonies in all compositions in order to express the emotions more completely.   The piano's construction was improved and it became THE instrument of the century.   Opera used new harmonies and rhythms but centered itself in the coloratura vocal line.   The Italian, Verdi, was thoroughly committed to the concept of grand opera that glorified the human voice, while the German, Wagner, represented the Romantic philosophy of being equally committed to voice and instruments.   He expanded the orchestra and gave them importance, though in designing several opera houses he had the orchestra out of sight.   This contributed to realism in the scenes and to the mystery and infinity of the harmony of his music.

In the latter 19th Century, love for native soil, comfort with native customs and tastes, and pride in native accomplishments led to the emergence of a recognizable national element in classical music. Composers made extensive use of native melodies and dance rhythms in their work.   Some of the more well know of these COMPOSERS are:

Bohemia - Smetana, Dvorak
Norway - Grieg
England - Elgar
Spain   -Albeniz
Finland - Sibelius
Russia   - Glinka, Tchaikovsky, Mussorgsky, Borodin, Rimsky-
                Korsakov

IMPRESSIONISM - Music at the turn of the 19th Century

As the 19th Century drew to a close, many of Europe's poor left for the New World, while the privileged and newly wealthy lived in a generation of peace and prosperity convinced they had created the highest form of civilization man had yet attained. Western culture was the center of the world: Paris was the artistic capital of Europe in a period called "La Belle Epoque" (the lovely time); in Austria, the elegant gaiety of the Viennese operetta epitomized the era; and in England, the Victorian period gave way to the Edwardian.

Like other aspects of life, dissatisfaction with old ideas and methods penetrated the arts. Artists began searching for new ways of expression which gave rise to several, most in the visual arts: impressionism, symbolism, and pointillism being the most important. As the Germans expanded their Romantic tradition and Richard Strauss became the dominant figure, the Italians continued in the operatic tradition, and nationalism continued in lesser countries. The French love of color began to interact with the arts and became the focus for a form of music that was in direct reaction to the Romantic ideal.

Impressionism in music sought to suggest sentiments and moods, to give impressions. The music appealed to the senses, was understated, and was less specific. Debussy was one of the first to achieve the new music. His "Prelude to Afternoon of a Faun" was described as "..preserving a feeling of elusiveness, of mirage: he attains it by the use of delicate unusual harmonies and by the silvery, web-like tracery of the phrases. The frequent use of the scale of whole tones and the unresolved dissonances produce a distinct charm of their own. The chords are of exceeding richness and present a depth of glowing color". (Demuth) Impressionistic music expanded the concept of key by weakening the pull to a tonic key and using the whole tone scale. Harmony was the principal means of composition (not form) and it introduced expanded chords of 9ths, 11ths, and 13ths. Ravel was another well know Impressionistic composer.

20th CENTURY MUSIC
The United States entered the 20th Century without a national heritage of music: each immigrant brought his own music, and the wealthy imported music from Europe. Although the American Indian offered a musical heritage, it was rejected out of hand. The Negro slaves, however, exerted a strong musical pull in the forms of ragtime and blues. And in 1917 an offshoot of ragtime developed into a style called jazz, which was characterized by a faster beat and an expanded melodic improvisation. There were also a few black men educated in the European style who endeavored to bring certain idioms of the Negro art into the mainstream of music. R. Nathaniel Dett was one of the most prominent men in this group. Mainstream popular music centered in a variety of types: operetta (Victor Herbert, Franz Lehar),

vaudeville (Cohan, Tilzer), Ziegfeld's Follies, Broadway shows (Irving Berlin), and parlor songs.

On the whole, the 20th Century has been one of rapidly expanding ideas and change. It is amazing to think back at the world just prior to WW I and compare it to the 1990's. It is said that 90% of all the inventions ever made have been produced in just this century! To accomplish this there has been an everpresent atmosphere of experimentation which has been fully represented in the arts. At the beginning of the 20th century, composers had been concerned with revising certain facets of their techniques rather than founding a new esthetic approach. More radical composers, the cutting edge, began to form the philosophy that most composers would eventually embrace: music produced from experimentation. The early avant garde composers began with changing the traditional harmony based on a triad and experimenting with other intervals including micro tones (smaller than the interval between a white key and black key on the piano). The composers were endeavoring to get people to use their ears in new ways. The emphasis was shifting away from the work of art toward the perception of the work of art that involved the listener.

Some of these early avant garde COMPOSERS were: Bartok, Hindemith, Stravinsky, Ives, Copland, Britten, and Schoenberg.

Music gradually moved away from a tonal center to atonality. When listening to this music there is no feeling of "coming back to home base" or of completion. In 1924 Arnold Schoenberg gave up the use of key signatures and wrote in the form call Serialism. Simply put, the twelve tones of the scale would be used with equal favor in a consistent order - music composed purely through intellect. Webern and Berg also became serialists and assisted in developing analytical systems to explain the working of serial structure.

Other composers were dealing with other techniques: Stravinsky explore new means within the old system: Copland reacted to serial techniques and incorporated folk music of the American frontier (barn dance, lonely open spaces, etc.) in his music; movies brought scenes of opera or orchestra to the public; musical theater flourished; and radio brought musical interludes, commercial jingles, theme songs, and sound effects to millions. Popular music of jazz and swing and boogie woogie took the country by storm.

In the 1950's technology entered the compositional world of music. Composers turned from disk recording machines to the magnetic tape recorder. And shortly thereafter the avant garde began experimenting with combining recorded music and/or sound with live music. At the same time the Germans were experimenting with synthesized sounds. The art of composing on a synthesizer involves manipulation of numerous variables of pitch, sound quality, duration, amplitude, attack and decay, etc, etc, etc., all based upon scientific/intellectual presentation of sounds. In 1954 Henk Badings won the Prix Italia for his radio opera "Orestes" which used synthesized sounds along with traditional music.

During the years of electronic music, traditionalists were continuing their experiments in two diverse directions. One direction was in extreme control in which Serialism took over rhythm and dynamics as well as the pitches. Messiaen, Boulez, and Stockhausen were the most well known composers of this form. The second direction was represented by the works of the American composer John Cage. He omitted (termed "pulled away") one seemingly necessary musical component after another. For example, in 1954 he "pulled away" sound itself in the composition "4'33". It consisted of four minutes and thirty-three seconds of silent contemplation of the open piano by the soloist. Cage worked toward "indeterminacy" in music: using random sounds, giving performers basic choices of procedure, and retaining only the specifications of overall length, locale, personnel, and instruments. He summed up his overall goal as "My purpose is to eliminate purpose".

Other composers used variables with less extreme goals. They used new sonorities with traditional instruments, i.e., blowing into instruments in varying ways; striking instruments; new vocal techniques; and changing the sound of a piano by adding materials in the strings. Notation of music needed to change to represent these new strategies and techniques. In 1964 the international summer music festival at Darmstadt, Germany held a special congress on notation resulting in a new book on notation. Attempting to read one of these scores is for most English speaking persons like trying to read Greek.

The late 60's and 70's brought a reaction to the atonality and extreme experimentation in the form of minimalism. This form, which is based in the traditional compositional forms, contains few melodies, harmony, and rhythm, but is based on constant repetition throughout. Not unlike other avant garde composers, Philip Glass found his compositions misunderstood until listeners realized nothing more was going to happen in the piece than the constant repetition. Letting go of expectations of forward movement and moving into the music allowed for a new meditational relationship.

The late 80' and 90's appear to be giving way to a return to spiritually composed music. Composers such as Goreski state have felt their music to have a spiritual dimension. It is also amazing the Goreski's Symphony #3 was number one on BOTH the classical and popular international charts in the early 1990's. In a time of world and individual crisis it appears that after decades of music composed for the sake of experimentation we are intuitively returning full circle to music that touches our spirits. At this point it should be clear how intertwined music is with mankind: with their religion/faith, with celebration, with physical outlet, and with intellect. And now deliberate attempts are being made to once again utilize this interconnectedness in the field of Music Therapy.

.

APPENDIX F

VIBROACOUSTIC MUSIC REFERENCES

1.Barlett, D. Physiological responses to music and sound stimuli. In D. Hodges (Ed.), Handbook of music psychology (2nd ed.) San Antonio: Institute for Music Research Press, 1996; 343-386.

2.Benson, H., & Klipper, M. Z. The relaxation response. New York: Avon Books, 1976.

3.Brewer, C. Boyd. The Somatron pain and anxiety management program. Tampa, FL: Somatron Corporation, 2000.

4.Brewer, C. Boyd, & Coope, V. Effectiveness of vibroacoustic music for pain and symptom management in outpatient chemotherapy treatment. In Proceedings of the First International Institute on the Arts in Healing, 5/ 16-17/03, Florida Atlantic U., Boca Raton, FL, 2000.

5.Brewer, C. Boyd. Vibroacoustic therapy: sound vibrations in medicine. Journal of Alternative and Complementary Therapies, 2003: 9(5): 257-263.

6.Brodsky, W, Sloboda, J A. Clinical trial of a music generated vibrotactile therapeutic environment for musicians: main effects and outcome differences between therapy subgroups. Journal of Music Therapy, 1997:34(1):2-32.

7.Burke M, Walsh J, Oehler J, Gingras J: Music therapy following suctioning: Four case studies. Neonatal Network ,1995;14(7):41-49.

8.Burke, M. Effects of physioacoustic intervention on pain management of postoperative gynecological patients. In T. Wigram & C. Dileo (Eds.), Music vibration and health, Cherry Hill, NJ: Jeffrey Books, 1997.

9.Burke, M., Phillips-Bute, B, & Vail, T. P. Positive effects of music therapy and vibration on satisfaction in TKA patients. Paper presented at the Department. of Veteran Affairs Second Annual Leadership Conference, 2001: Pain Management and End of Life Care, Alexandria, VA.

10.Burke, M., & Thomas, K. Use of physioacoustic therapy to reduce pain during physical therapy for total knee replacement patients over age 55. In T. Wigram & C. Dileo (Eds.), Music vibration and health (pp. 99-106). Cherry Hill, NJ: Jeffrey Books, 1997, 99-106.

11. Burke, M. A. Feasibility of physioacoustic therapy in cancer care. Unpublished report NIH Grant #1 R43 CA 75899 - 01 A1, 1996.

12. Butler, C., & Butler, P. Physioacoustic therapy with cardiac surgery patients. In T. Wigram & C. Dileo (Eds.), Music vibration and health. Cherry Hill, NJ: Jeffrey Books, 1997; 197-204.

13. Cass, H., Slonims, V., Weekes, L., Wigram, T.& Wisbeach, A. Therapy services for Rett Syndrome: how well does provision match specific needs? Paper presented to the Royal Society of Medicine, London, 1993.

14. Chesky, K.S., & Michel, K.E. The music vibration table (MVT): developing a technology and conceptual model for pain relief. Music Therapy Perspectives, 1991;9 32-37.

15. Chesky, K.S. The effects of music and music vibration using the MVT ä on the relief of rheumatoid arthritis pain. Dissertation Abstracts International, 53(8), 2725B. UMI No. AAC9300593), 1992.

16. Chesky, K.S., Michel, D.E., & Kondraske, G. Developing methods and techniques for scientific and medical application of music vibration. In R. Spintge & R. Dron (Eds.), Music medicine: Vol 2. St. Louis: MMB Music, 1996;227-241.

17. Chesky, K S, Russell I J, Lopes Y, Kondraske G. Fibromyalgia tender point pain: a double-blind, placebo-controlled pilot study of music vibration using the Music Vibration Table. Journal of Musculoskeletal Pain. 1997;(5)2:22-52.

18. Clair, A A, Bernstein B. The preference for vibrotactile versus auditory stimuli in severely regressed persons with dementia of the Alzheimer's type compared to those with dementia due to alchol abuse. Music Therapy Perspectives, 1993;11:24-7.

19. Curtis, S.L. The effect of music on pain relief and relaxation of the terminally ill. Journal of Music Therapy, 1986;23(1), 10-24.

20. Darrow, A A. The effect of vibrotactile stimuli via the Somatron on the identification of rhythmic concepts by hearing impaired children. Journal of Music Therapy, 1992; 26(3):115-24.

21. Hodges, D. Handbook of music psychology. Dubuque, IA: Kendall Hunt Publishing, 1980.

22. Hooper, J., Lindsay, B. The use of the Somatron in the treatment of anxiety problems with clients who have learning disabilities. (1997). In T. Wigram & C. Dileo (Eds.), Music vibration and health. Cherry Hill, NJ: Jeffrey Books, 1997; 169-176.

23.Hooper, J. An introduction to vibroacoustic therapy and an examination of its place in music therapy practice. British Journal of Music Therapy, 2001;5:69-77.

24.Hubbard, S. J. A study of rapid mechanical events in a mechanoreceptor. Journal of Physiology, 1958;141, 198-218.

25.Jindrak, K., & Sing, H. Clean your brain and stay sound and sane. Forest Hills Station, New York: Karel F. Jindrak and Heda Jindrak, 1986.

26.Lehikoinen, P. The physioacoustic method. In T. Wigram & C. Dileo (Eds.), Music vibration and health. Cherry Hill, NJ: Jeffrey Books, 1997;206-216.

27.Llina, R., & Ribari, U. Coherent 40-Hz oscillation characterizes dreamlike states in humans. Neurobiology, 1985;90, 2078-2081.

28.Lundeberg, T. Vibratory stimulation for the alleviation of chronic pain. Acra Physiologie Scandinavia, 1983;523 (Suppl.),1-5.

29.Lundeberg, T. Long-term results of vibratory stimulation as a relieving measure for chronic pain. Pain, 1984a;20,13-23.

30.Lundeberg, T. The pain suppressive effect of vibratory stimulation and transcutaneous electrical nerve stimulation (TENS) as compared to aspirin. Brain Research,1984b;294, 201-209.

31.Michel, D. E. & Chesky, K. Music and music vibration for pain relief: standards in research. In R. Spintge & R. Dron (Eds.), Music medicine (Vol. 2), St. Louis: MMB Music, 1996; 218-226.

32.Ottoson, S., Ekblom, A., & Hansson, P. Vibratory stimulation for the relief of pain of dental origin. Pain, 1981:10, 37-45.

33.Patrick, G. The effects of vibroacoustic music on symptom reduction: inducing the relaxation response through good vibrations. IEE Engineering in Medicine and Biology. March/April, 1999;97-100.

34.Patrick, G., Burke, M. & Lipe, A. A systematic review of recent vibroacoustic therapy research. Unpublished manuscript in review, 2003.

35.Quillian, T. A., & Sato, M. The Distribution of myelin and nerve fibres from Pacinian corpuscles. Journal of Physiology, 1955;129, 167-176.

36.Skille, O. Manual of vibroacoustic therapy. Levanger, Norway: ISVA Publications, 1991.

37.Skille, O. The effect of music, vocalization and vibration on brain and muscle tissue: studies in vibroacoustic therapy. In T. Wigram, B. Saperston, & R. West (Eds.), The art and science of music therapy: a handbook. Amsterdam: Harwood Academic Press, 1995.

38.Standley, J. M. The effect of vibrotactile and auditory stimuli on perception of comfort, heart rate and peripheral finger temperature. Journal of Music Therapy, 1991;28 (3), 120-34.

39.Vincente, P., Manchola, F., and Serna, E. The use of vibroacoustics in idiopathic Parkinson's disease. In T. Wigram, B. Saperston, & R. West (Eds.), The art and science of music therapy: a handbook. Amsterdam: Harwood Academic Press, 1997.

40.Walters, C. The psychological and physiological effects of vibrotactile stimulation via a Somatron on patients awaiting scheduled gynecological surgery. Journal of Music Therapy, 1996;33(4), 261-287.

41.Wigram, T. The feeling of sound-the effect of music and low frequency sound in reducing anxiety in challenging behaviour in clients with learning difficulties. In H. Payne (Ed.), Handbook of enquiry in the arts therapies. London: Jessica Kingsley Publications, 1993;177-197.

42.Wigram, T. The effects of vibroacoustic therapy on clinical and non-clinical populations. Unpublished doctoral dissertation, St. George's Medical School, London University, 1996: http://quadrillo.tripod.com/~quadrillo/index-4.html

43.Wigram, T. The effect of VA therapy on multiple handicapped adults with high muscle tone and spasticity. In T. Wigram & C. Dileo (Eds.), Music vibration and health, 143-148. Cherry Hill, NJ: Jeffrey Books, 1997;143-148.

44. Wigram, T. Vibroacoustic therapy in the treament of Rett Syndrome. In T. Wigram & C. Dileo (Eds.), Music vibration and health). Cherry Hill, NJ: Jeffrey Books, 1997;149-155.

45.Wigram, T. & Cass, H. The role of music therapy in a clinic for children and adults with Rett Syndrome. Paper presented to the BSMT Conference, London, 1995.

About the Author

Born to a nurse and instrumental music teacher, Suzanne's destiny was set from day one, although it took her decades to realize it. Her school years were focused on music, learning to play several instruments and participating in many music groups including a semiprofessional orchestra. Her Bachelors Degree is in Music Education which she used briefly to teach instrumental music grades 4-12 in East Central Connecticut. After several years of diversion as a costumer in several theaters and teaching at the Universities of Connecticut and Massachusetts, she went back to music focusing on music and healing and behavioral medicine. Her doctoral dissertation study was on using music with one-day surgery patients.

She has applied her music medicine in several general hospitals and rehabilitation facilities, a pain control clinic, pulmonary program, a women's health care center, and a fertility institute. She is a 23 year faculty member of the Creative Education Foundation which awarded her their highest honor, the Outstanding Leadership Award in 1987. She has been active in the professional division of The Monore Institute, and is a regular trainer with the American Holistic Nursing Certification Program through BirchTree.

She is currently the director of the Inner Harmony Health Center in Maryville TN focusing on the use of music, sound, and energy for healing. She regularly teaches a training course in music medicine for healthcare professionals, is a frequent conference presenter, and has authored several audio tapes/CDs for healing. Her *Deep Relaxation/Self Healing* CD was chosen by National Public Television in 2003 as a pledge premium. Her publications include a chapter on Music Therapy in *Physical Medicine and Rehabilitation: the Complete Approach* (11/99), and contributing columns on the MindBody Connection to various newspapers. She has served as national vice president of the Wholistic Wellness Network (www.wholisticwellnessnetwork.com).

She invites readers and practitioners to share their experiences with her at:
www.InnerHarmonyHealthCenter.com